ANTHOLOGY

SHORT STORIES I

First print edition: Sydney 2018
First ebook edition: Sydney 2018
Publisher: Sydney School of Arts & Humanities
15-17 Argyle Place Millers Point NSW 2000
www.ssoa.com.au

ANTHOLOGY Short Stories I
ISBN 978-0-6483216-3-7 (print book)
ISBN 978-0-6483216-4-4 (ebook)

Copyright ©Editors: Christine Williams & Maria Issaris and ©Contributors: Cat Davey / Jennifer Neil / David Benn / Matt Jackson / Stewart Adams / Rossco Robertson / Sam Herzog / Matthew Stuart / Marjorie Banks / Sharon Dean / Grace Lightly / Richard Hambleton / Lawrence Goodstone / Carolyn Thrum / Clarissa Militante / David Adès / Guy Micklethwait / Geetha Waters, 2018.

The moral rights of the above authors being identified as authors of single stories included in this work have been asserted in accordance with the Copyright, Designs and Patents Act, 1988. All rights reserved. Without limiting the rights under copyright reserved above, no part of this publication may be reproduced, stored in or introduced into a retrieval system, or transmitted, in any form or by any means (electronic, mechanical, photocopying, recording or otherwise), without the prior written permission of both the particular copyright owner above and the publisher, Sydney School of Arts & Humanities. Nor may it be otherwise circulated in any form of binding or with any cover other than that in which it is published by this publisher as an ebook or a print book, without a similar condition being imposed on the subsequent purchaser.

This is a work of fiction. Names, characters, businesses, organisations, places and incidents are either the product of the authors' imaginations or are used fictitiously. Any resemblance to actual persons, living or dead, events, or locales is entirely coincidental.

Cover design and formatting Ferdinando Manzo.
Typeset Times New Roman
Printed and bound by Lightning Source, 2018.

National Library of Australia Cataloguing-in-Publication data: ANTHOLOGY Short Stories I/ Editors: Williams, Christine & Issaris, Maria. Contributors: Cat Davey / Jennifer Neil / David Benn / Matt Jackson / Stewart Adams / Rossco Robertson / Sam Herzog / Matthew Stuart / Marjorie Banks / Sharon Dean / Grace Lightly / Richard Hambleton / Lawrence Goodstone / Carolyn Thrum / Clarissa Militante / David Adès / Guy Micklethwait / Geetha Waters, 2018.
ISBN 978-0-6483216-3-7

Contents

Foreword	9
An Architect's Dream House	15
Cat Davey	
An Innocent's Guide to Hitchhiking	25
Jennifer Neil	
The Worst Day of My Life	33
David Benn	
Across the Dark	43
Matt Jackson	
An Accidental Acquisition	59
Stewart Adams	
The Card Flick	67
Rossco Robertson	
A Girl	83
Sam Herzog	
Refuge	97
Matt Stuart	
Mara Immaculata	111
Marjorie Banks	

A Skyful of Stars	121
Sharon Dean	
Vengeance and Betrayal	133
Grace Lightly	
Cynthia's Last Foxtrot	143
Richard Hambleton	
The Reverend Timothy's Temptation	161
Lawrence Goodstone	
Words for Sam	177
Carolyn Thrum	
Cecilia's Kind of Love	193
Clarissa Militante	
The Bare Bones of a Story	203
David Adès	
Taxi Driver	215
Guy Micklethwait	
A Trail of Marigolds	225
Geetha Waters	

FOREWORD

It is with great pride and pleasure that Sydney School of Arts & Humanities (SSOA) presents to the reading public this our first short story anthology, as part of our expanding publications list.

SSOA's primary aim is to nurture emerging writers through attendance at our writing meet-ups, specialist classes and mentoring sessions – and we are committed to the publication of high quality works by our members.

Yet this anthology goes even further, matching the storytelling skills of our emerging writers in the meet-ups – Sydney Writers Circle and Sydney Storytellers – with those of new writers in other parts of Australia and Asia. Our goal to search for the best of emerging writers' works may account for the stimulating range of fictional voices showcased in this collection. About half of the contributors to the anthology have attended writing groups at the School, and the other half responded to a call for submissions through our website: www.ssoa.com.au.

It's vital to a writer's sustained skill development to be published, and a pathway leading to such an achievement is becoming increasingly difficult in Australia with the contraction in the number of print journals, newspapers and literary presses. We are therefore delighted to provide this publishing opportunity for those writers who have been selected from among the many submissions received. Their tenor and writing styles range from the literary to the colloquial.

A sharp and witty study of modern manners – or lack of them – is at the core of Cat Davey's story, *An Architect's Dream House*. Intelligent, stylish and just plain funny, it's a piquant view of middle class surprises. Just as humorous is Sam Herzog's story, *A Girl*, which may well set your nerves on alert, as fantasies of dating are viewed through the lens of gritty inner-city life.

David Benn's *The Worst Day of my Life* offers wry humour and philosophical musings, along with lawyers and schooners. And this all in the context of telling a tragic tale – with Aristotle hauled in to make a singular point.

A Skyful of Stars is an intimate and expressive piece of writing, playing with notions of memory and poetry as a means of posing newfound perceptions of the world. In this story, Sharon Dean pushes the boundaries of what creative expression is in essence, particularly when intellect becomes weakened.

Across the Dark by Matt Jackson is a mesmerising story exploring the emotional terrain shared by a man and a boy on a car trip. Mystery, memory and a restrained spartan style lure the reader ever deeper into a family secret.

The humour and compassion of Stewart Adams' travel

story, *An Accidental Acquisition*, are a treat – marrying emotion with vividly described adventure, all written in a fluent engaging style.

A completely different type of travel story again is Jennifer Neil's hitchhiking adventure, which describes the pitfalls of being young, adventurous, and carrying a large backpack of naïveté. *An Innocent's Guide to Hitchhiking* will take you to a time and place that you'll wish you had known and shared. Dry, crisp and engaging writing at its best.

Clarissa Militante's story about adolescent love and longing, with its many twists and turns, has a multinational setting. In *Cecilia's Kind of Love*, the mood verges bravely on the territory of youthful behaviour driven by yearning and the unexplored drives of childhood. By contrast the vivid characterisation of Cynthia in Richard Hambleton's *Cynthia's Last Foxtrot* carries a message about the sharp sting of time's whip hand, and how one feisty woman deals with it.

No anthology would be complete without a dystopian tale, which Matt Stuart handles with nail-biting precision in *Refuge*. Read on for intrigue in the nature and behaviour of people caught on the cusp of world-changing events.

Would you recognise a holy person if you met one? In *Mara Immaculata*, Marjorie Banks carries us into the thoughts of an apparently simple and honest person, whose life takes an extraordinary turn. Insightful and surprising, it's masterfully written with a touch of suspense.

David Adès lyrical tale, *The Bare Bones of a Story*, is folkloric in nature, exploring love, loss and promises made and kept. It may even be conceived as a tower, drawing people into its heart-driven themes.

Another youthful tale with a serious underscore is the schoolyard adventure, *The Card Flick*. Told with Rossco Robertson's usual enthusiasm and skill, the story contains the best of suspense, drama, and the type of character study that only a child's view can elicit. Think Huckleberry Finn, Australian schoolyard-style. Exhibiting similar insight into character, Lawrence Goodstone's *The Reverend Timothy's Temptation* is a study in the varied shades of venal sin, and the tricks of light that temptation plays on the morals of even the most decent of human characters.

In *Vengeance and Betrayal*, Grace Lightly describes the trials of choosing the option of an 'open relationship' in the current dating scene – with an unexpected gap between theory and practice for the colourful and clever main character.

A secret language becomes the binding glue for a family torn apart by tragedy in *Words for Sam*. In true iconic Australian style, Carolyn Thrum describes the fortitude and resilience of a small girl at the centre of a drama.

Over-qualified, under-employed and in debt, the protagonist in Guy Micklethwait's story *Taxi Driver* is forced to drive passengers around Sydney for a quick financial fix. But all too soon, taxi driving thrusts the hero into the peccadilloes of the city's street life after dark.

Finally, a rare and insightful glimpse of rich Indian culture – the language deceptively simple and lyrical – is found in the last story of our collection, *A Trail of Marigolds*. Geetha Waters discusses the commonplace nature of death in the midst of natural beauty and grandeur.

Members of Sydney School of Arts & Humanities invite you to take the time here and now to savour the delicious fruits of our authors' writing prowess.

Dr Christine Williams & Maria Issaris – Editors
Ferdinando Manzo – Publication Text and Cover Designer

AN ARCHITECT'S DREAM HOUSE

Cat Davey

Susan removed every last item of her husband's belongings out of the family home in an exaggerated succession of throws, like a toddler having a tantrum. Ted was banished.

At first he telephoned and left phone messages. He always defended himself in the same way: he was manipulated, he had no intention of repeating it. But Susan remained white hot for much longer than it took for Ted to give up on trying to win his wife back. After three months he had moved across the country to Galveston, had opened a practice designing beach houses, and then within six months he had taken up with a new woman, a homely nurse called Judy, who didn't consider Ted's single transgression anything more than an interlude of not unnatural curiosity.

And although Susan instantly fell out of love with her husband, the feelings that followed were not just regret and grief but a festering bitterness that never relented. It wasn't just the act of infidelity, but the humiliation of that particular someone he had betrayed her with. Susan felt that her family's status, her personal standing in the community was sunk by her husband's actions. She never again appeared at the school. She drove 30 miles from home to shop at a supermarket where she wouldn't have to endure the stares or looks of pity. And with each duck and dive to avoid embarrassed stares or sympathetic inquiries, her bitterness deepened.

For Kimberley, her father's indiscretion was a double blow. The man who was meant to love her unconditionally had not only betrayed her love but ruined her status at school. The magical gaggle of cool girls that had been at her side quickly departed. While her mother had orchestrated a withdrawal from the community to avoid the embarrassment, Susan did not extend the same option to Kimberley. Since it was her final year of school it was decided that she must endure the remaining six months at Fielding Secondary School. And if Kimberley was to describe her life during those six months it was in one word - sniggers - which was the kind of scornful laugh that teenagers were able to deliver with a deftness that no other age group could. As she turned into corridors, entered classrooms, emerged from her locker, standing at assembly and once, as she passed the open door of the school staffroom, Kimberley was subject to sniggers.

The day Susan's life began to change had started like most others. At breakfast Susan passed the butter to Pedro, the Spanish exchange student, aged eighteen, his tanned hand brushing hers as he accepted the glass dish. His dark collar-length hair was glossy in the morning sunshine that blazed through the French doors of the kitchen. He smiled and two perfect dimples appeared. Ted was reading the paper and did not see the moment Pedro licked his knife. A long sensual lick, the kind of action a woman might find a flirtation, an invitation. But Susan, who had found Pedro's overt sexuality at first astounding, then unsettling, for a boy who had only just left school, could not abide the licking of a knife. The conspicuous disregard for table manners annoyed her even as he was staring at her smiling, with those bovine eyes of his, a gooey brown with lashes too long and lustrous for a man. She sucked in a deep breath and contained the urge to huff. Her daughter Kimberley, on the other hand, was gazing intently at the glide of tongue on knife. Kimberley, Susan noted, had entered a kind of trance when Pedro, a year older than Kimberley, had arrived in their home.

They would listen to music in Kimberley's room. He played guitar, with his shirt unbuttoned to just above his waist. Smooth brown skin over toned muscles rippled downwards and disappeared into his jeans which were pale and low slung. He would swim in the family's pool, wearing not the long polyester shorts of Kimberley's male classmates, but what Susan called his 'continental' costume, hugging a smooth package of something that looked proportionately too large for his teenage trimness.

'I think that Pedro is going to try to have sex with Kimberley,' Susan said as she lay in bed that night next to her husband.

'What makes you think that?' Ted asked.

'Have you not seen the way he licks his knife. He's practically having sex with that piece of cutlery. He's trying to seduce her.'

'He's just like that. I don't think he has a particular thing for Kimberley. He's just …' and Ted paused while he searched for the right word, '... European.'

'Helen and Buck Partridge's German exchange student Claus is not licking cutlery or having sex with his eyes and he's European.'

'That German boy has cystic acne and is still reading Harry Potter.'

'Well, that's not the point. I think you should have a fatherly talk to him.'

'What shall I say to him: stop licking the knives?'

'How about, "Don't take our daughter's virginity"'.

'Susan, I think it would be naive to think she's still a virgin. She's seventeen.'

'Of course she is. She's my daughter and that's how I've brought her up.'

'OK, I'll have a chat with him. But don't blame me if it doesn't achieve anything.'

Susan resumed the planning of her day as she usually did by talking through her upcoming appointments in bed as Ted lay reading. He rarely commented except to mention a shirt that may need a button sewn on or an upcoming absence due to a work commitment he alerted her to.

'I'm going to the market right after breakfast,' Susan informed him. 'I need to get everything done before Kimberley's dress rehearsal at 11. I'll probably grab lunch with Barb and then I'll be scooting over to the house at 2 o'clock to meet the contractor. You remember?'

'Yes, I've got that in my diary. I'll see you there. And when you're at the market can you get me some more of that Pritikin muesli,' he said rubbing his stomach, that was only slightly larger than when they had married 25 years earlier. Since Pedro had offered to be his personal trainer, Ted had dropped ten pounds and the muscles Susan had last seen when they were both in their twenties had started to resurface.

The new house was in its late stages. Dry walling had begun and Susan was planning to discuss final finishes with the contractor. A palette of baby blue and cream swatches were sitting on her sofa, waiting to be taken to the house tomorrow. Ted was an architect. He had designed the house with three gables, a turret, a four-car garage, a faux Tudor facade – a giant affirmation of his career. This, his grandest vision, was to be settled in his own home on Long Island. The result was just a smarter, larger version of the homes he designed for his suburban clients at his practice. His style wasn't avant garde. Ted did not aspire to win any architectural awards. A good home, in his professional opinion, should survive another civil war, should not challenge city building codes, and made no apology for its dependence on tradition.

The next morning at the grocery store, Susan glided her trolley into the cereal aisle.

'Why, Susan, Susan, hello honey.' It was more a coo than a tone of greeting. Even though the voice was coming from behind her, Susan knew instantly the voice belonged to Candy Shaw, a woman with small hips and large breasts, which the school mothers had unanimously concluded were silicone. Susan turned around with a smile already on her face. Candy was wearing white stilettos. Honestly, thought Susan, stilettos at age forty-eight, to go grocery shopping?

'How are you, Susan? I haven't seen you for so long.

How's the family?' Candy enquired.

'We're all doing well. Ted is busy. Kimberley is very busy socially these days, quite busy.'

'I bet she is,' Candy said with a smirk. 'And how's that young Adonis you've got living in your house, you lucky thing.'

'Oh, he's enjoying life in America.'

'I bet he is,' Candy said again, and this time she winked. 'We'd love to see you and Ted and the kids sometime. We're having a BBQ on Sunday afternoon. Cherry and Cam will be there. Pedro should see a real American BBQ – John is roasting a whole suckling pig. You really should come.'

'Well, I'll have to ask Ted. He's always making plans and not telling me.'

'Oh sure. Let me know.'

Candy pushed her trolley forward and Susan grabbed the cereal her husband had ordered. It was invitations like these that made Susan realise Pedro had become Kimberley's personal mascot, a tool to incite the jealousy and fascination of her less worldly male classmates and a magnet for the female ones and sometimes their mothers. Kimberley's diary had suddenly become jammed with invitations to picnics, parties, hiking, rock climbing, horse riding, concerts. All these events Kimberley was invited to, and now the family, were in the name of offering Pedro a real taste of American life. But everyone knew the real intent was the chance to interact with the handsome brazen Pedro.

After Susan arrived at Kimberley's school she made her way to the assembly hall and took a seat with a dozen other parents who were allowed to watch their daughters in the dress rehearsal. Kimberley emerged from the wings. At first she strutted in the spikey high heels she was wearing, then jigged a bit to the beat of the Supertramp song, *It's Raining Again*. She suddenly opened an umbrella she was carrying and began to spin it as she walked. But her enthusiasm for walking like a model was greater than her skill. She faltered and looked down to steady herself.

'Eyes up, look straight ahead, smile,' said the voice of a woman over a PA system that was too loud for the hall that was nearly empty. The dress that had been chosen for her was fitted, short and fire-engine red. The umbrella matched the colour of the dress. It was the kind of dress Susan would never let her leave the house in. Without makeup she looked too young to be wearing it, but Susan knew that when the fashion parade for the school fair was held for real on the weekend, the make-up, applied by beauty salon owner Candy, would fast forward the look of her young face to meet the outfit. Barb entered the hall just as her own daughter Margot marched out. Barb was Susan's closest friend among the school mums. They were around the same age with daughters who were both tall thin figures, unformed and flat like boards.

'Those dresses, outrageous,' Barb announced as she hugged Susan. Margot was modelling a similar dress to Kimberley's but it was black and only slightly longer.

'Oh yes, terrible. Hardly covered the vajayjay,' Susan agreed.

'I think that's the idea.'

'Are you ok?' asked Susan as she noticed Barb was clutching a cold press to her cheek.

'I've got a toothache. I'm booked for the dentist and can't make lunch today. Can we take a rain check?'

'Sure,' said Susan. Kimberley appeared in her own clothes and announced she was taking Pedro to the mall after school.

'Ok, but be home by six for dinner, no later.'

With time to kill Susan decided to head to the new house early, to take some time to fantasise about her upcoming life in pastels before the contractor and her husband arrived. She parked the car outside and walked around the back, picking her way past long planks of wood, downed tools and other building paraphernalia. But before she reached the back door, she could see that Ted was already there. He was standing in the kitchen, with his back to the wall. It was the wall where Susan had planned to have top-of-the-range dual wall ovens installed. Ted eyes were closed like he was in pain. No, it wasn't pain. Susan looked down and there was the head of someone. It was level with Ted's groin, doing something.

Susan froze while she tried to fully cognise the scene before her. Then slowly, deliberately, Susan grabbed a circular saw that sat on a table outside the kitchen. Heaving it above her head with both hands, she threw it into the kitchen, smashing the newly fitted glass doors in the process. She then grabbed the next available item, a drill that sat on the same work bench and threw that too. Then she picked up a large ladder. Hardly able to balance it, she nearly dropped it before vaulting it at the doors. And then she found some planks of wood. Rubble and dust made visibility poor so only Ted's voice could be heard.

'Susan, Susan, what's going on?' he said as he emerged

from the dust, walking towards her, a trickle of blood running from his head. He was holding his hands waist high, with palms up like he was simultaneously declaring his innocence and gesturing his surrender. Ted's companion was nowhere to be seen. But Susan did not stop. Ted ducked as a box of nails came flying, hit him in the chest and scattered.

'Get out of my house, get out, get out, get out, both of you get out,' Susan roared. The person she had seen at her husband's groin was not a woman sucking her husband's cock, but a man. And the man was not a man, but a teenager. That teenager was Pedro.

AN INNOCENT'S GUIDE TO HITCHHIKING

Jennifer Neil

In 1963, I was living in digs in London with two friends. We all had boring jobs, and were going crazy trying to find two shillings to put in our small gas heater every ten minutes.

I was so cold at night I went to bed in my duffle coat.

Desperation drives people to do outrageous things, so my friend Joan and I decided we would 'hitchhike through Europe' for a change of scenery. Without any knowledge of hitchhiking, Europe, or where we were going, we set off from London, each with a small suitcase on wheels, the wheels strapped on with leather bindings. We both had £60, our hard-earned salaries from our jobs, and that was all. Our unrealistic thinking was that it would be enough, as staying in youth hostels only cost us 2/6d a night, and as it cost 13s/6d to cross the English Channel, we felt rich.

We decided to make our way to Austria and Italy. Coming from South Africa, we had never seen snow, and so far London had only produced a rainy slush. In my naive way, I wanted to go tobogganing, and roll in the fluffy white stuff. What fun that would be!

The quaint little village in Austria we were staying in looked exactly like a chocolate box painting. It was a pleasure to go outside and just stare at the massive amounts of snow, which made the buildings seem smaller, as all doorways had a portico over the entranceway. Joan and I rushed about excitedly not knowing how to experience it all.

Next day we rented two toboggans, then asked the way to the toboggan run. I wondered why people were looking at us in such a strange way. Never having seen snow, let alone having tried tobogganing, we took a ski lift to the top of a mountain, bursting with confidence.

Reaching the top, we noticed there were no other people around. An icy track that looked like a bush track, except covered in snow and ice, led down the mountain. I have always been unafraid to try new things, so I hopped on my little wooden coffin of death and took off.

The toboggan set off slowly at first, then gathered speed downhill in a straight line, gathering momentum until the first bend in the track. Then at that first bend, the trusty toboggan continued on its own trajectory in a straight line, over the edge of the mountain, and I landed about 100 feet down below, in a pine forest.

I seemed to be alive, but my body was in pain and numb with cold and fear. I crawled back up the steep snow slope, dragging the death machine behind me. When I got to the top, I saw Joan peering down at me with a look of horror on her face. Unlike 'Miss Brave Heart', she did not even attempt to use her toboggan. I was sitting on the edge of the track feeling sorry for myself when two boys aged about fourteen appeared. They offered to take us down the mountain and tied our toboggans to the back of theirs, so Joan and I both got on the back of their toboggans.

They literally flew down the mountain. I was terrified. They hit huge bumps in the snow and the toboggans took off in the air before landing, with me hanging on to one boy so tightly he could hardly breath. When we got to the bottom, about a mile down, Joan and I both looked like people who had had a great shock. My face was white and my hair was actually standing up. Joan looked even worse. The grinning teenagers seemed to get a great kick out of our looks of terror, as we staggered away.

After few days of freezing snow, we decided we would like to go to Italy, so we started our serious hitchhiking phase. We stood on the side of the main road out of town, with hundreds of other hitchhikers nearby, all going to Italy.

Out of nowhere, a large truck stopped in front of us with two men aboard, a driver and his mate. They were going all the way to Milano and could give us a lift to the outskirts.

Great! Joan jumped in next to the man who was sitting next to the driver, and I sat next to the door. After about half an hour, with little conversation, the man next to Joan put his arm around her shoulder and stuck his hand into her blouse, resting his hand lovingly on her rather large breast. He just sat there, continuing to talk to his mate, as if this was a normal truck driving thing to do. Unfortunately, Joan had a very bad habit of smiling when she was nervous, so the man thought she was enjoying it. A frantic discussion ensued between Joan and me, going something like this:

'Tell him to take his hand off you,' I said.

'I don't know how to say it in Italian,' she said

'"NO!"' is the fucking same in every language,' I shrieked.

The two men just kept up their conversation as if nothing was unusual, with the guy's hand still firmly clasped around Joan's ample bosom. Joan still had her idiotic nervous grin on her face, and he must have thought, 'Well, she's having a wonderful time! I might try a little squeeze.' This produced a nervous squeak from Joan, but Mr Italy had a huge grin on his face. He was having a delightful time, probably with a fantasy anticipation of a sojourn to be spent later with this buxom wench.

Eventually I shouted, 'Stop,' so they obligingly did and we got out, the men looking surprised that we did not want to accompany them all the way to Milano.

With the whole of Australia, New Zealand and South Africa hitchhiking on the roads we were travelling on, lifts were now impossible to get, so we decided to catch a bus. We walked a long way in the snow to a bus stop, and hoped the next bus would go to Milano. We had reached the top of the mountains from Austria so it would be downhill all the way.

Finally, a bus came down the road and stopped with a screech of breaks. I noticed that it was full of little old ladies decked out in black head scarves, all going to the next town to shop. It was nice to be welcomed by these strong women of Italy. They all joined in greeting the two of us, 'Buongiorno Signoretti'. It was so relaxing not to be worried about who had whose hand on whom. The women all chatted to us as if we were part of their community. Then suddenly, the bus driver started driving very fast, and the women were shouting and yelling for him to stop his reckless driving. I was really nervous, imagining all sorts of fatal endings to this bus trip. The driver beckoned to Joan and me to come and sit up in front with him. I refused, and the bus women started a high-pitched screaming at him, with a lot of words like *morte* being thrown about.

At last the bus stopped at a small village and the driver jumped out, beckoning Joan and me to follow him. We both sat in our seats telling him through the window that we were going to Milano. He became quite hysterical, shouting at us to get out, and making signs with his hands that we should have a drink with him. That's when our women's solidarity group in black decided they had had enough. It appeared obvious to us that the camaraderie of the women had evaporated. They were now shouting at us to get off the bus. We did not want to upset the old ladies, so off we went. The bus driver then rushed us over to a bar and ordered three small glasses of some white liquid, one glassful of which he swallowed down in a mouthful. He did a bizarre dance, shaking his whole body. We both refused his drinks, so he then proceeded to swallow both of ours. This produced another ridiculous weird dance of firewater performed by him in the street. The women on the bus were now in an uproar, yelling at him to get back on the bus and drive them to their destination. I was very determined I would not go another inch with him. He staggered back on the bus and took off at great speed. Our last sight of the old ladies, was of their black heads jerked backwards by the driver's reckless speedy start.

We had had nothing but bad experiences all day, so we decided to try hitching again, after my discussion with Joan about who we would take lifts from in future. It was decided we would only take lifts from people in motor cars, after seeing what they looked like before getting into the car. Good, now we had a plan.

We stood on the side of the road for about an hour and a little Fiat came slowly to a stop and Joan had a look in. A little old man got out with difficulty. He let Joan in the back with a pat on her bum and turned around to me, saying, 'No. Uno, uno.' He drove off, with Joan's smiling nervous face staring out the back window.

This presented a huge problem for me. Where was he taking her? How would she find her way back to me? Should I start walking, hoping she would be strong-willed enough to get him to stop? Would I ever see Joan again? I did not even know where I was because the name of the last town was an absolute blank in my mind as a result of the crazy bus driver's behaviour.

I decided to start walking in the direction the car had gone. I was angry with Joan for just jumping in the back without me. She had looked at me as if there was nothing she could do about the situation, except give a nervous smile and wave. I would have liked to think she was not waving but throwing her hands up in panic, but that would have taken a stretch of imagination.

I walked for about an hour with rising dread when I suddenly saw her strolling along towards me. God, I was so glad to see her. She entertained me with how she had to hit the old man on the back of his head to get him to stop and, even then, he pinched her bum on the way out of his small car.

Then, as the sunny afternoon gave way to fading light, I was thinking how all that had happened constituted just the first day of our spontaneous, expectantly-gleeful hitchhiking adventure.

THE WORST DAY OF MY LIFE

David Benn

'It is during our darkest moments that we must focus to see the light.'
Aristotle

'Mate, that fuckwit Aristotle was a fuckin' fraud!'

I was being poked in the chest by Andrew, my family law solicitor, in the crowded public bar of the Civic Hotel opposite the family law courts late in the afternoon on the worst day of my life.

Up until this moment there had been several worst-day-of-my-life scenarios.

The first was when I was ten years old. It involved my embarrassed parents, angry neighbours, broken windows, stern policemen and my air rifle. That day was surpassed in my teens when the worst day of my life involved me, a bottle of Bundaberg Rum and several school friends ploughing a parent's new car into a muddy drainage gully late at night on a remote farm. That day was, in turn, superseded in my twenties when the worst day of my life involved the loss of nearly two million dollars, my removal from my role as a derivatives dealer in a prestigious foreign bank and the public humiliation of being paraded out of the dealing room by senior bank management.

However, here I was on the cusp of middle age having experienced the ultimate worst day of my life. This involved Andrew my family law solicitor, an ageing world-weary registrar, my ex-wife and her big fat Greek solicitor.

My ex-wife and I had been divorced for over a year and had yet to reach agreement on a financial settlement and parenting orders. To avoid the matter going any further, adding to a mountain of back-logged cases, we were to meet at the Family Court on Goulburn Street in Sydney in an effort to negotiate a settlement.

Early in the day, the ageing world-weary registrar had sat behind her large wooden desk in her office, looking at the four people in front of her from behind large dark-framed reading glasses. She had told them in a dry, monotone voice that if they didn't achieve financial settlement and agreement on parenting orders that day she would schedule the ensuing court case two years ahead, and would ensure it lasted at least three days and would cost both parties one hundred thousand dollars.

With no parenting orders in place, I had only been able to see my five year old boy on the sporadic whim of my ex-wife ever since I'd moved out of the family home over two years before. My ex-wife's latest boyfriend had moved in with her and my child. She had taken to making my little boy call him, 'Dad'. I was missing him terribly.

I looked across at the three people sitting beside me. Andrew was young, with chiselled features and blonde hair swept back. Dressed in his blue suit and crisp white shirt, he cut a handsome even heroic figure as if penned by F. Scott Fitzgerald. My ex-wife's big fat Greek solicitor sat in her knee-length brown skirt and matching brown jacket, her black hair pulled back into a bun. There was a light moustache under her large nose. And finally there was my ex-wife. She had lost a lot of weight recently and her skin was drawn tight across her face, her long brown hair was pulled tight into a ponytail and her lips were tightly pursed as she glared at the ageing world-weary registrar.

We all walked out of the registrar's office towards the negotiating rooms. Andrew and I took one of the small white-walled windowless offices. My ex-wife and her solicitor took an office nearby. Negotiations commenced with my ex-wife and me sitting in our small rooms giving our solicitors instructions and they, in turn, met outside in an open plan area, sitting on a faux leather couch next to a plastic indoor plant, to negotiate the terms.

Financial settlement was straightforward enough and by midday we had agreed all the assets would be sold and the proceeds shared between us. Andrew was feeling buoyant.

'Parenting orders are pretty straightforward too. We should be out of here by two o'clock,' he said.

But agreement on parenting orders was not straightforward and my ex-wife refused to negotiate on any access other than one weekend a month.

Her solicitor tried to convince her that any court would grant me access of every other weekend, one night during the week and half the school holidays. It wasn't worth going to court over. Andrew did his best to charm my ex-wife into accepting more reasonable access. My frustrated ex-wife raised her voice and told them she was not moving on this issue.

By three o'clock, Andrew was sitting in our small room leaning back in his chair. His hands were behind his head, his jacket was off and his sleeves rolled up.

'You know, mate,' he said in a matter-of-fact voice, 'we could try to buy our way out of this. If you go to court you will get access to your child but those parenting orders will be two years away and afterwards you may not be left with any assets.'

'That's right,' I agreed.

'Well, if you offer her some money and assets now, then after today you may very well end up without assets but at least you will have final parenting orders and access to your child.' Then Andrew leant forward and looked me in the eye. 'If you work hard you will make more money. If you save that money you will buy back those assets. But you will never buy back that time with your child.'

I told Andrew to offer the assets. Andrew stood up, rolled down his sleeves and pulled on his jacket. He ran his fingers through his swept-back blonde hair, straightened his back and walked out of our small room to offer my share of the assets to my ex-wife in exchange for access to my child and so avoid going to court.

But my ex-wife refused our offer. Her solicitor strongly advised her to accept the offer. My ex-wife started yelling in exasperation. Andrew threatened to withdraw the offer. Then, my ex-wife screamed at her solicitor she wanted to file for sole custody. My ex-wife's big fat Greek solicitor stared at my ex-wife in incredulity.

'I'm sorry, Rachel. A court will only grant sole custody if a parent is absent never to return or is a missing person or something like that.'

Andrew turned on his heels and left my ex-wife and her big fat Greek solicitor to sort that out for themselves. He walked back into our little room and flung his jacket on the table. He loosened his tie and undid the top button of his shirt. He put his elbows on the table and held his head in his hands. His eyes were dark. 'Mate, I want to go home. We can come back another day and work through this.'

'Andrew, I don't want to relive this day. I'm sorry but you're not going home until we have parenting orders or we are asked to leave.'

And there we sat in our little room looking at each other, both wondering what to do next. Until there was a faint tap on the door. Andrew opened it to see my ex-wife's somewhat dishevelled big fat Greek solicitor.

'Okay, my client will accept your offer. We will agree to custody every other weekend, half the school holidays and other days as set out in the parenting orders you put forward in exchange for the house, the car and half of your client's superannuation.'

'What made her change her mind?' Andrew quizzed.

The solicitor sighed and shook her head. 'I told her if she proceeds with this sole custody nonsense and doesn't settle today then I could no longer act for her and she would have to find herself another family law solicitor.'

At 4.30 the four of us walked back into the world-weary registrar's office. Andrew tabled the signed parenting orders.

My ex-wife's solicitor tabled the signed financial settlement and some other papers, including the results of a paternity test.

The meeting was brief and heart-breaking. My ex-wife walked out with the assets. Her big fat Greek solicitor walked out with the money. Andrew and I walked out, across the road to the public bar of the Civic Hotel and started drinking.

And there I was on the worst day of my life, after several schooners and whiskeys, looking at the happy young legal types around me and listening to my now somewhat bedraggled family law solicitor defame the father of western philosophical thought and reason.

'We all know Aristotle's first book of Poetics was all about tragedy. Right?'

I nodded in agreement.

'And we all know after he wrote it his old mate Plato came to see him and told him he was being miserable and needed to write something with a bit of levity. Right?'

I nodded again.

'And so we all think he went and wrote his second book of Poetics which was all about comedy, right?'

I nodded yet again.

Andrew stopped poking me in the chest and pointed his finger in the air. 'Only he didn't actually write a second book of Poetics. All he did was change the title of the first book, hand it over to Plato and say, "There you go".' Andrew took a sip of whiskey. 'We've been looking around for the last thousand years or so for this second book of Poetics about comedy and the fuckin' thing doesn't exist.'

I frowned at Andrew. 'What makes you think he just

changed the title?'

'Because I do it all the time. In all my years as a family law solicitor I have only ever written one parenting agreement. The first one. After that all I've ever done is change the names and dates on the document and negotiate my way around it.'

I raised an eyebrow.

Andrew noticed and rolled his eyes. 'Yes, mate, even yours,' he said without apology.

Still frowning, I said, 'But Andrew, tragedy and comedy are very different.'

'No, they're the same thing. The only difference between tragedy and comedy is circumstance and perspective.'

'Sorry, Andrew, I'm not sure I agree with you.'

'Well, tell me if this is comedy or tragedy. In the late nineteenth century one of the first African American law enforcement officers in history goes to a small town in the western United States but is set upon by the inhabitants and is nearly lynched.'

'That is a tragedy.'

'But that is what is portrayed in Mel Brookes' 1974 film *Blazing Saddles* and it is still regarded as one of the funniest movies ever made.'

I was in no mood for flippancy and shook my head. 'Life is just not like that, Andrew.'

'It is, mate. Even today had its moment of humour.'

I dropped my lower jaw and stared at Andrew in amazement. 'There was nothing humorous about today in any way, shape or form. It was all tragic.'

'There was comedy. But only at the end.'

I put my whiskey on the bar. I couldn't believe what I was hearing. 'Andrew that was the worst five minutes of the worst day of my life! As much as I love that little boy and am thankful I now have parenting orders, I had to hand over my assets to gain those orders. Then, having done that, I was handed a paternity test proving the child wasn't mine! Everything about that is tragedy!'

'Yes, mate, it was a tragedy for me too. But then I turned around and saw the look on your face. And suddenly it was pure comedy.'

ACROSS THE DARK

Matt Jackson

I leaned against the passenger side of my car and smoked a cigarette while I waited in the midday heat for the kid to come out. I could hear his parents talking inside. The murmur of their voices drifted on the still air, muffled and indistinct, like a leaf touching the surface of water.

That was okay. I could wait.

The house looked alright. The weatherboard's paint cracked and peeled like old bark, and an unfinished brick entryway framed a screen door you might find in a scrap yard. The front lawn bristled green, though, and a concrete driveway that led to the garage still carried a fresh sheen. Better than my place, that's for sure. Real suburbia. I took another drag of ash and cast my gaze over this picture before me.

The clatter of the door opening centred my attention. The kid stepped out, a cap shielding his eyes as he came down the steps. A couple of figures hovered in the doorway behind him. His mother laid a hand on her husband's arm, a frown worrying her face; the man watched me as you might a drunk stumbling towards you.

They didn't matter though. With limp fingers I dropped my cigarette into the gutter.

The kid wore a baggy shirt that hung from his shoulders as if from a clothes rack, and a pair of torn, faded jeans. With every step his feet scuffed grass. Even halfway across the lawn I could see from the shape of his cheeks, slim though they were, that he had his mother's dimples. He looked at me, sharp green eyes – these from his father – hunting like a hawk's.

He stopped a foot away from me. We considered each other.

'Hi,' I said.

'Hi.' His voice cracked, pitched sharp at the end.

I offered my palm. 'I'm Danny.'

'Paul.'

We shook. Then stared at each other, suspended like two motes of dust drifting in a beam of light.

'You wanna get going?'

Paul nodded. 'Yeah.'

I walked around to the driver's side and got in, then unlocked the passenger side door across the front seat. Paul opened the door and hunched forward to sit, then hesitated. He straightened, turned, waved to his parents once, barely a flick of his wrist. Then he ducked in. The door thudded shut behind him.

My piece of shit car hadn't been serviced in a decade so needed a start to get going. On the third try the engine roared to life, before settling into a deep, primal rumble. Paul looked at his home as we pulled away, head tracking back over his shoulder. Once it passed out of sight behind us, he turned his gaze to the windscreen.

Both of us kept our attention on the road while I negotiated the streets. The family lived in an old part of town, the paths so tight only one car could pass at a time. The engine's rolling thunder would have drowned any noise we might have made speaking. I found my way onto the main arterial road, Industrial Drive, and pushed up our speed.

We had just cruised past a semitrailer, in a high enough gear finally to smooth the motoring of the cylinders to a low growl, when I spoke. 'Your parents end up deciding I'm not a paedophile?'

The kid looked down at his hands curled in his lap. 'Almost.'

'Almost?'

'I think so. Mum didn't like it.'

'But?'

'The government lady said it was ok.'

'That's good.' We sat there silent a few moments.

I cleared my throat. 'So, you still go to school?'

In the corner of my vision Paul's head stiffened and turned a fraction. 'Yeah.'

'You like it?'

A smirk curled his lips. 'Nuh.'

My smile mirrored his. 'Yeah. Didn't like it much when I went.'

We paused again. I glanced at him. 'Long left?'

He shrugged. 'Couple of years.'

Attention back on the road. 'Any plans once you're done?'

He grunted. My heart sank, pulling the corners of my mouth down with it. I scratched my nose and pretended I held a sneeze. Fuck. I grasped mentally for something else to say but my probe found nothing, just that single curse echoing around inside my skull.

Paul saved me then. He cleared his throat and, phrasing each word carefully, said, 'A lot of people have a gap year. So I reckon I'll do that. Have a gap year.'

I nodded, but my well of conversation remained dry. The questions I'd prepared seemed suddenly fake, stupid. I didn't dare try winging it. Paul returned his quiet gaze to the passenger window. I kept mine deliberately forward. The car's frame rattled. The silence settled between us like dog shit.

I turned off Industrial Drive and onto an island strip, Kooragang, part of a line of cars in single file. The thick shrubbery to our right faded to a dusty strip of grass. To our left the marsh gave way to a massive open construction site and, beyond a chain-link fence stretching the length of the road, great hills of coal blackened the sky. The greenery on our right came to an end. A loading terminal hosting a queue of enormous cargo ships took its place.

My attention kept being pulled sideways. Paul drew my eye like a magnet, a physical presence as conscious to me as my own hands. In the margin of my sight I watched him observe the changing scenery.

I realised my jaw was clenched. I inhaled slowly, forcing it to loosen on the next breath out. Rolling my arse in my seat, I slipped a hand into my back pocket. In painful increments I took out a pack of cigarettes. I knocked the top open and, with a flick of my thumb, ejected a butt from the pack. That end I held up and slid the rest of the way out with my mouth. Then I lit up, drawing long as I hunched over and wound down my window, then drew in again when I swapped the cigarette to my right hand. I rested my forearm on the open frame and let the haze swirl in my lungs.

'Can I have one?'

My head jerked around as if caught stealing. It'd been less than a minute but I'd completely forgotten Paul while I sorted myself out. He stared straight at me.

I held my cigarette between my lips. 'Sure,' I said, around it, and passed him the pack. I divided my attention between him and the road, fighting down a grin while he tried to light up. He bent his head to the cigarette, holding it between the first two fingers of one hand, with his lips pouted around the butt and his body hunched like a vulture. He held it still while he touched the lighter flame to its end then took an experimental puff. When he realised the cigarette hadn't caught he brought the lighter back up. Again, it didn't take. His cheeks began collecting heat.

I waited until we hit a straight stretch of road. 'Here.' I took the steering wheel with my right hand, my own smoke sticking vertical between my knuckles, an oily coil rising from the tip, and reached over to Paul with my left. 'Put it in your mouth.'

When the cigarette jutted from his lips I flicked the lighter to life and held the flame to the charred tip. 'Breathe in.' When it caught, apart from being obvious by the acidic melt burning towards him, the lines of his body shifted as though he was furiously listening for something.

I let the lighter die and dropped it in the drinks holder. Paul took several quick drags, his birdcage chest puffed out. I grunted, 'Roll down your window.' After he did that, his slight frame near making it a full body exercise, I asked, 'Your first?'

He shook his head once, curt. 'Nuh.'

'Right. Your parents know?'

He said nothing.

'What would they think?' I pressed, only mildly curious.

He shrugged. 'Doesn't matter anymore, hey.'

As I turned into another suburban area set with rows of lazy houses I bounced that around my mind. I let it go. Nothing off my back. I stole a sideways glimpse at him and changed tack. 'You have a girlfriend?'

Paul breathed out the window, smoke tearing away in a thin stream. 'No,' he said quietly.

'Boyfriend?'

He spluttered, choked on his cigarette. He managed a brief 'No' before dissolving into a fit of coughing.

I laughed. 'You right, son?'

He nodded and wiped his mouth with the back of his hand.

'I mean, not like it's a bad thing,' I said. 'It's just …'

'No,' he cut in, hoarse. Then, 'No. There's a … this girl.'

'Ah. You're not together.'

'No.' He looked back out the window. 'I don't wanna talk about it.'

'Sure,' I said, gently. I took another drag of my cigarette. Not wanting the conversation to die I asked, 'You play any sports?'

He did of course – his parents had told me earlier – cricket and Union. I knew the games well enough, but their mention sent a volt through Paul. In the space of five minutes his walls fell from without. He spoke rapidly, gesturing with both hands and bouncing in his seat, telling me about the playing moves, trash talk and fights.

Turned out he surfed too. When he mentioned it I asked if he'd like to stop by the beach and he nearly grabbed the wheel himself, he was so keen. So I did a U-turn and backtracked a way. After realising that going to the movies had a bit of a weird vibe to it, I hadn't suggested it, instead driving around aimlessly. But driving nowhere hardly seemed better. Our surfing connection cut that problem and stopped it gnawing on my mind. On our way I stopped to buy pies and two bottles of Coke. The scrunch of paper bags and slap of open-mouthed chewing filled the rest of the ride.

A few quick turns later, we arrived. Finding a place to stop proved easy enough. A level road spanned the beachfront, nice looking houses on one side, a small strip of grass on the other. Beyond that the beach stretched away in a sandy crescent. A yellow arc separated land from sea and, apart from the long white streaks the breakers out back left on the water's surface, nothing broke the deep blue's tint. Over it all hung a bright sky, fluffy white clouds floating high above – a pretty picture. A cool breeze teased my hair as we left the car.

We crossed the road and walked onto the grass, Paul chatting while I finished my pie. A jumble of heavy stone blocks divided the grass and sand. We headed there. I popped the last of the pastry into my mouth and crushed the paper bag, wedging it between two stones. Then I climbed onto the pile of blocks. After a moment's hesitation, Paul followed.

Our conversation fragmented while we crawled about, halting and punctured with grunts. It didn't take long to find a spot we could both sit comfortably. Straight away Paul looked out over the ocean, alert as a mastiff on the hunt, pointing out the different breaks and the movements of current and tide. I asked how he knew, which launched us in a new direction that ended with a frank, albeit tentative, discussion of climate change. We smoked a few more cigarettes together.

Eventually our strangerhood caught us up, though. Our back and forth settled into a lull. We sat in silence, the ocean spread wide before us. As the sun warmed my skin, the heat sinking into my muscles, I closed my eyes against it and allowed the knot between my shoulders to relax.

'You knew my Mum, didn't you,' Paul's voice asked beside me. 'I mean, my real Mum.'

I opened my eyes and turned to focus on him across the gap between us. He stared at the ocean still, his brow casting pools of shadow that hid his eyes. I followed his gaze. 'Yes.'

'What was her name?'

'Irene.'

A storm might have passed through the pause that followed. Then, hesitant, 'What was she like?' and he spoke in such a small voice that all the pieces of my heart tore a little more.

By way of answer I shifted my weight to more easily get my wallet. Paul turned as I flipped the fake leather open and took a fold of photo paper from inside. The outside edges of it wilted and curled, and it fuzzed so badly along the creases you could almost see light through the wear. I opened it as if pulling apart the petals of a flower, then passed it to Paul. He took it with velvet hands and held it in his lap.

In the picture a young woman was holding a baby. The photo caught them mid-laugh, the baby with a pure, wide-mouthed glee, tiny arms clutching his mother's. I focused on her though. Always did. She had a diamond-shape face, a dusting of freckles spreading from the peak of her nose outwards across her cheeks, all her features soft except her smile. That, matched by her dimples, might be mistaken for a moment's cheekiness instead of a glimpse at her deepest personality. Around her eyes gave the appearance of bruised gauntness, yet despite this, captured even in the picture, the blue of her irises sparkled like buried treasure. Two small elfin ears poked up on both sides of a slick ponytail, a small ring piercing the top of her left ear's helix.

Paul's resemblance to her was obvious. There were differences of course: his mop of hair was much thicker than hers, their eye colour and skin complexions differed, and the slope of her cheeks was slightly sharper. Yet next to her image, he might've been her younger brother.

I shifted my gaze to Paul. His face looked drawn as if by age or long hours working a ditch. He searched the image like he might find some meaning hidden behind it.

I watched him a while, leaving him to his own small sphere of privacy, then turned away towards the ocean. I waited a bit longer. Then I began.

'She was the best person I ever knew,' I said, low enough

to keep my voice between us. 'She was always there for everyone else, even when she was busy. Most people you can't depend on to reply to a text in a couple hours, but with her you'd be unlucky if you had to wait five minutes. Never had a bad word to say about anyone. Always gave her all. But she was fun to be around too, knew how to enjoy herself, have a good time. She could've been the world's best comedian if she'd tried. Saw the good in everything. She loved life. Truly.'

Fuck me! Fifteen years later and I still broke. Tears streamed down my cheeks, blurring my vision, tickling my chin where they fell. 'When she had you … it was the happiest I've ever seen her. It was like somebody took the light inside her and turned it into an exploding star. She loved you, Paul. If you ever wondered. She loved you more than anyone.'

A movement caught my attention. Paul had remained hunched around himself while I spoke, immersed in his silence. He lifted his head now, though, moving as if made of stone. His eyes stayed on the picture until the last possible moment. Then they flicked up and locked on me. It scared me, the intensity to them. 'What happened?'

I tried to bring myself to meet his eye, couldn't, and found my bootlaces instead. I took a shuddering breath. 'She got killed. Murdered, I guess.' I rubbed at my eyes with the heels of my palms. 'There was this guy who got completely obsessed with her. She'd known him before, dated him for a bit. Called it off when he started getting weird. He was jealous. Possessive. Must've blown a fuse or something when she left, 'cause he started stalking her. Went through her mail, called her and her friends day and night, rocked up to her work.'

I shook my head. 'Kept getting worse ... Cops wouldn't do anything, of course. Said he hadn't done anything wrong.' I spat. 'Anyway, she was back with her ex by then – her real boyfriend – and he was around but they were fighting again. Some stupid shit. Him being a dick, really.'

I paused, pushing that word, the condemnation, around my mind, before quietening my voice another notch. 'Not long after you were born, six months maybe, he broke into her house. She was home by herself. Cops said they argued for a bit. Then he took a knife and stabbed her.' I left out the rest of what he'd done. 'There was nobody else who could look after you so you got put with a foster family. He went away for life. Ended up killing himself in jail. And that was it.'

After I'd finished Paul's stare went past me to the distance beyond. He blinked rapidly, his lips slightly parted. His head dropped back towards his lap. The distant sound of a wave rushing up on the sand washed over the silence, then receded into it once more. I fumbled for another cigarette and stuffed it in my mouth. I offered the pack to Paul. He didn't look around or say anything, didn't do more than flick me away with the back of his hand.

Finally he raised his head. 'What about my dad, then? I mean ... I had a dad, right?'

'Yeah.'

'Was it this guy?'

'No.'

'What happened to him then.' Again, that intensity. 'Why didn't he take me?'

I chose that moment to clear the ash from my mouth with

a long drink of Coke. I screwed the cap back on, tightened it. Took another drag from my cigarette. Blew it out, took a breath of fresh air, clenched my guts at the words forming on my tongue. 'Like I said, he and your mother had been fighting. The sort of thing you normally forget ever happened. They still loved each other. When he found out she'd died, he was devastated. It destroyed him.'

I raked a hand through my hair. 'I don't know why he didn't take you. Maybe he felt guilty about the fight. Or maybe he lost it after that, wasn't fit to parent.' I stopped, and when I spoke again went on in little more than a murmur. 'But I reckon it's 'cause he'd really been in it for her. Seen you as a part. Something to do with her. And he couldn't stand the idea of raising you by himself. It'd remind him of her every single day.'

Paul sneered at his shoes, his upper lip curling back from his teeth savagely. 'I fucking hate him,' he spat.

I glanced at him sharply. 'You don't like your family? Your parents?'

'No, I do! It's just … like, how could he leave me like that?' He looked down again. 'We're supposed to be family.' He scuffed his shoe against the rock with a small, violent kick, then added, soft, 'He's a dog, mate. A fuckin' dog.'

I faced back towards the ocean. 'Yeah,' I murmured. 'Can't argue with that.'

We stayed a while longer, both of us drained and not much else going on in the way of words. Eventually I checked my watch and suggested I get him home.

Paul grunted his assent. 'Here,' he said. Solemn, as if

making a religious offering, he returned the picture to me.

I asked him if he wanted to keep it, or at least get a copy, but he shook his head. I put it back in my wallet. Neither of us spoke a word on the ride back. He held his head out the passenger window the whole way, eyes closed and hair whipping in the wind.

Parked out the front of his house, we shook hands like we had on first meeting. 'It was good to meet you, matey.'

'Yeah. You too.' He let go.

'Maybe we'll do this again sometime.'

'Yeah. Maybe.'

We sat there half-turned to each other. 'Alright,' I said, the word dropping like a stone. 'Well. See you.'

'Seeya,' Paul said. He got out of the car, crossed the front lawn, and went inside. I watched him go. I stayed a minute longer, staring at the house. One of the front curtains was pulled back a fraction, then resettled. The rear view mirror threw my eyes back at me, red raw around a pair of green bullseyes. I started my car and pulled away.

I drove back the way I came, retracing the route to get Paul home. The scenery I passed blurred into a single indistinct portrait, a smear of blues and greens and browns. Soon enough I found myself cruising along the beachfront again. I parked and headed over to the stone wall.

It didn't take long to find exactly where we'd sat. Our scattered rubbish and a small pile of cigarette butts marked the spot. I scrabbled over to Paul's rock and settled in where he'd been. For a few minutes I picked out the breaks and currents he'd shown me, committed them to memory. Then I took out the picture of Paul and Irene once more and let it lie in my lap.

As always, my eyes lingered on her, soaking up her image, drowning myself in each tiny detail. This time though they faltered, drifted, fell onto the boy. Perhaps for the first time ever, I really saw it, the two of them together. The iron banding my chest drew tighter.

I looked at the photo a long time, its edges feathery fine between my fingers. I thought about tearing it up, setting it on fire, scattering the pieces and ashes to the wind. In the end I didn't. I was crying again.

With a heavy sigh I took my pack of cigarettes from my pocket and opened it. I dipped my fingers in. Found only air. I looked down and saw that it was empty. I stared into the bare pack for several long seconds. Then, giving a snort, I dropped it down with the other rubbish.

I stayed a while longer, watching the blazing orange of the horizon bleed deeper, first crimson, then purple, the light's reflection on the water turning to oil. In the last of the dying sun's rays, I took one long final look at the picture. 'We'll meet again,' I murmured, before I got up, went to my car and drove away.

AN ACCIDENTAL ACQUISITION

Stewart Adams

The greatest stories are often the worst experiences. At least that's what I tried to tell myself as I stared at the smoke rising from the engine of my quad bike. I scanned my surroundings for help but there was nothing but fields, overgrown with grass and the odd tree here and there. Then there was SoPat, my Cambodian guide. His smile belied all confidence in my abilities to sort this out. I sighed.

The day had started off so well. I had hired the quad bike from a Frenchman who didn't hesitate to tell me how wonderful Cambodia was and why he'd immigrated there. I had only been in the country a few days so I just smiled politely until I could escape and find SoPat. He was a small man of all smiles and little English.

After we'd picked up our bikes for the day, I'd looked with some scepticism at SoPat's patchwork scooter. Yet after a bit of spluttering, the bike coughed into life, sending a small cloud of petroleum-reeking smoke into the air. I'd started my own quad bike, which hummed nicely, and we were off. It didn't take long before the tall buildings, crowded streets and paved roads of Phnom Penh gave way to the countryside's dusty dirt roads, mazes of rice fields and quaint thatched houses. As we rode, I was jostled and jolted along the tangle of dried river beds that had once been their roads, but it did give Cambodia an air of wild and untamed beauty.

Every village we rode through, the children would line the road like some sort of honour guard, holding out their hands so we could high five them as we flew past. Their ragged and dirty appearance was a sharp contrast to the enjoyment they were clearly having. To see them was infectious and I was laughing as I high fived them.

Before I knew it, we were pulling up to a wooden house, raised off the ground to avoid the floods of the rainy season. It sat on the banks of a picturesque ancient river that swept ahead and out of sight. SoPat led me through some trees that lined the river and down to a dock. The cooling breeze rolling off the water was a welcome change to Cambodia's oppressive heat. SoPat sat down on a mat with his legs bent behind him. The wooden beams creaked alarmingly as I tried to emulate his posture but quickly gave up. I wasn't that flexible.

SoPat rubbed his stomach and pointed at the house, which I assumed meant lunch. I just hoped it wasn't some of their more traditional dishes such as fried tarantula or spiced crickets. I was relieved when it turned out to be a delicious roasted duck with steamed rice and a pot of gravy. A short man who delivered our lunch was approaching old age. SoPat greeted him with his hand clasped to cover his mouth and then moved his hand above his head. It was a sign that was reserved for monks and respected elders. As we ate, the man began speaking about his childhood. While I knew it was part of the tour, I couldn't help but be moved by the man's story as he relayed, in broken English, the harrowing times when the Khmer Rouge had raided his village.

I was only seven years old at the time. My father woke my brothers and me. We could hear the rumble of trucks in the distance, then their headlights shone through the slats in the walls. He told us to move quickly. I started to cry and my father hit me on the side of the head, telling me to be quiet. He rarely hit me. I followed him beneath our house. There our mother and sister were already crouching. My mother was a strong woman but she looked terrified. I can still see how scared she was. We could hear the men pouring out of the trucks and the clink of their rifles as they burst into the village houses. I didn't fully understand what was happening and, again, I started to cry. My father tried to make me be quiet but I wouldn't. So he grabbed me and said if I didn't be quiet, he would throw me outside and I would never see them again. I had never seen my father like this and while I wasn't happy, I kept quiet. I could hear the soldiers' military boots thudding through our house. The men shouted loudly at each other and I saw some of my friends and neighbours herded into the courtyard. There they were put into the trucks and I never saw them again. Eventually the soldiers left our village, but we stayed in our hiding spot until morning.

The next day we saw the other families. Everyone

but ours had some members of their families taken. We never found out why they were taken. It was at that point that my father took our three books and burnt them. He made us swear to never tell anyone that we could read. He then took my sister's glasses and broke them, throwing them away because glasses were a sign of schooling, something they would kill us for. Our village was raided several more times over the coming years and they would always take more people who were never seen again. I don't know what became of them but I assume they are dead. Even after the Red Rouge force was defeated, my mother would never allow me to go to school. She was too scared that they would kill me for learning to read. We survived and now I have a family of my own. But not many families were as lucky as we were.

He finished his tale. My appetite was gone. The three of us sat in silence. Sometimes that's all you can do.

Three days earlier I had visited the torture centre S-21 and the nearby 'Killing Fields' where a large part of the genocide had taken place. Over two million Cambodians were killed during the four-year reign of the Khmer Rouge. One quarter of the population had been massacred for no greater reason than they could read or were related to someone who could. It horrified me then and hearing about it from someone who had lived through that time made it terrifyingly real.

SoPat had to nudge me back into the present. The survivor had already left. I rose and followed SoPat, my mind lost in a melancholy daze. We returned to our bikes and started back, my guide leading the way. The countryside was a blur as my thoughts focussed on the Pol Pot genocide. So much so, I hadn't noticed SoPat had stopped. I slammed on my brakes, narrowly avoiding crashing into his scooter.

We had stopped at a high school. Typical of Cambodian architecture, the walls were low and the roof was high to allow a natural draft of cool air. SoPat pointed at himself and at the sign that arched over the entryway. I followed my guide as he led me through his old school grounds.

As the teachers stood in front of their classrooms using chalkboards to teach Maths and English, it was hard to believe that the mass genocide had occurred less than forty years ago. We walked past a sewing class and there was even a group of students huddled around a single laptop being taught computer studies. The students wore immaculate uniforms. That seemed a miracle in such a hot and dusty country. While they smiled and joked quietly amongst themselves, they were far more well-behaved than I remembered the students of my high school years.

We made our way to the rear of the school where the seniors were playing volleyball on a red dirt court, dressed in clothes that looked like they came from the discard pile of a thrift shop. I followed SoPat to watch their game more closely, dodging the live chickens and walking around the school's vegetable gardens. Despite their small stature, the kids played with an enthusiasm and skill that would rival professionals. At the end of one of their games they invited SoPat and me to play and I realised that even when I used to play competitively, I would have been completely outclassed by them. But they never made me feel unwelcome, laughing at both my triumphs and fumbles. We bowed out after a few games, not wanting to overstay our welcome, and got back on the road towards Phnom Penh.

The tree cover thinned and I could feel the sting of the sun on my face as we sped towards the next canopy of cover. Then the bike lurched so suddenly I almost hurtled over the handlebars. I tried to regain my seating and unconsciously revved the engine. A sputter of fire burst from the engine before shrouding the bike in a veil of smoke. I nearly fell over myself in my haste to get off the bike and turned off the ignition before retreating, just in time to watch the slow death of my transport.

Once the smoke had subsided a little I looked at SoPat, hoping he could moonlight as a mechanic. He shrugged at me. I took a glance at his scooter but quickly dropped the idea of him doubling me. The thing barely carried my guide, and he was half my size and weight. There were only fields, scattered trees and dusty trails near us. Phnom Penh was a ridiculous distance away. I waited for the smoke to subside completely and, thinking there was nothing else for it, I sighed, put my hands on the handlebars, pulled in the clutch and started pushing the bike.

I had reached barely more than a kilometre when I stopped for the first time. I tried to wipe the sweat off my forehead but the rest of my body was just as drenched in sweat. The heat was a constant, oppressive blanket and my throat was so dry it felt like someone had lodged a knife in there. I took a few minutes to recover before pushing again but I only made it another few hundred metres before I had to stop. Phnom Penh looked further away than ever.

Then SoPat rode a few hundred metres up the road, got off

his scooter and came back to help me push. We continued this system for close to another kilometre. We were passing an ox farm when we paused again. These animals were much thinner than the stereotypical ox but I had seen many pull heavily burdened wagons. I stopped, an idea bubbling in my mind to use an ox to tow my bike back to Phnom Penh. I turned to SoPat and after some confusing charades, I eventually got the idea across. SoPat went over to the owner who was lying comfortably in a hammock.

The ox farmer approached me with the standard Cambodian smile and despite the language barrier, we started to barter. After lengthy dickering, we settled on $40 USD, a ridiculous sum by Cambodian standards. But it was one I was willingly to pay if it got me back to Phnom Penh so I could return the bike and get some of my deposit back. We tied the bike to the ox and I led it along the dusty paths, broken and overgrown roads, and dormant river beds. Sweaty, miserable and disgruntled, I arrived back at the shop long after sundown.

The shop owner apologised profusely for the all the hassle that the broken bike had caused. I waived him off, saying these things happen, and trying to get in his good graces so that I could leave the ox in his care. But when I asked if he could return the ox to its owner, he spoke to SoPat and after a moment burst out laughing. It took some time for him to regain his composure and explain why he was laughing. The reason I had paid so much for the ox was that I hadn't hired anything, I had bought the god damned ox.

As I stared at my new purchase I wondered out loud, 'What the fuck am I supposed to do with you?'.

THE CARD FLICK

Rossco Robertson

My best mate Chad leans over to me. 'You sure about this, Scott?' I hear the question, but I choose not to answer. I am unsure. I feel uneasy. I want to pull out. I want to go back in time and change what I did, but I can't, not now. I have to face it, simple as that. Maybe, just maybe there will be some type of miracle. As that thought enters my mind, I hear thunder rumbling in the distance …

Card flicking began for me halfway through Year 2 at primary school. I remember seeing kids flick cards around the schoolyard. It looked fun and intriguing. It wasn't until I was taught by my older brother who was in Year 4 at the time that I officially became a card flicker.

Now I am in Year 4, my brother Mal is in Year 6. We are similar in looks with fair hair and a collection of freckles across our cheeks and nose, but Mal is a seasoned card flicker, and he is known around West Pymble primary as one of the best.

Technically you can card flick any type of card. For us, it's trading cards, also known around card flicking circles as collector cards. Trading cards vary, from basketball cards or Rugby League cards to Teenage Mutant Ninja Turtle cards. Almost any popular sport, TV show or movie will have a series of collector cards to go with it.

Any spare pocket money we have is most likely spent at the local newsagents buying a pack of seven cards that come with a standard stick of pink bubble gum. Opening the packet of cards to the smell of the gum is almost as much of a joy as discovering what seven random cards you've just purchased. You always hope for that one card you don't have or that ultra-rare card that is very, very hard to get. For me, I always spend my hard-earnt pocket money on Teenage Mutant Ninja Turtle cards. I'm going for the set and I am only about ten cards away. The next best thing to having an ultra-rare card is to have a complete set.

The little fame I have around West Pymble primary school is that I have one ultra-rare card. It is the Teenage Mutant Ninja Turtle Cowabunga card. It is rare, and I own it, I'm the only one at school to have this card. It is my pride and joy and is by far the most valuable item I own.

When adults ask us how to play the game, we tell them you put a trading card in between your index finger and middle finger, with the card facing toward you. You raise your hand back toward yourself, then you throw your wrist quickly forward, and when it reaches the right position in front of you, you release the card, 'frisbeeing' it forward. Your card flies through the air and should land quite a distance in front of you, as far as possible to win the game.

Everyone has their own unique flicking style. Some kids run into the flick, others swing their whole body to give the wrist more momentum, some aim the card toward the ground, others aim high. When my brother Mal and I flick, we flick to win. There are a group of guys at school who are the best at card flicking, and my brother Mal is one of them.

Competing in a card flick is simple. You challenge someone any age or skill level. You put your card up against theirs and whoever flicks their card the furthest wins the loser's card. It can be a cruel game, but everyone is aware of the consequences of accepting a challenge. One thing about card flicking is that even the smallest and youngest kids can become heroes of the schoolyard for a day by winning a card flick where the odds were heavily against them.

Not long after the start of this year, a new kid arrived at school. He got everyone's attention straight away. He had slick black hair and would wear sunglasses during recess and lunch. His name was Brock and he entered the card flicking circles on his very first day.

Brock had a card that almost every kid at West Pymble primary wanted. It was a New Kids on the Block holographic card, really rare. And what made it even more unique was that it was signed by all five members of the band. Everyone would challenge Brock for the card and everyone who challenged Brock lost. He was a master in card flicking, he could flick his card twice the distance of the best card flickers we knew in West Pymble. Challenge after challenge just meant a win after win for Brock. He was a legend. But there were a few things that didn't sit right with me about Brock. He would only ever flick using the one New Kids on the Block holographic card, and he would never, ever, let anyone touch his card.

After about six months, Brock had let his 'undefeated' status go to his head. He was known as the card flicking 'Kingpin'. He walked around the schoolyard like a card flicking hero, and pretty much believed he owned the schoolyard. People began challenging him not because they wanted his card, but purely because they wanted to be 'the one who defeated Brock'. It was simple. If you went up against Brock then you were going to lose no two ways about it. It surprised me that he still had challengers every day. Fools, I called them.

The recess bell rings. Chad and I are eager to get to the schoolyard quadrangle. It's the middle part of the school bordered by classrooms that have a covered walkway connecting each class. The principal's office and the main entrance to the school are next to the eastern section of the quadrangle and on the northern side sit the canteen and the sports sheds. The quadrangle is covered in pebblecrete on the ground, and there are chairs and bins scattered about. All card flickers assemble out the front of the library. The section of the quadrangle from the library across to the sports shed is the longest section of the entire quadrangle and perfect for card flicking. Even though no one has reached the sports sheds with one flick, it's the dream target for everyone, with only Brock coming close a few times.

'Scott and Chad, can you two stay to help me, please?'

Our exit through the classroom door is halted by our teacher, Mr Day. On Thursdays after recess our class has art and Mr Day always asks a couple of students to help with setting up the classroom for the lesson. It's a responsibility shared among all students, but today Chad and I draw the short straw. It means we'll miss most of the recess card flicking.

Chad has been my best mate since pre-school and we pretty much share the same interests: V shows, comics and Where's Wally books. Chad has blonde hair styled as an under-cut. He has a habit of tucking the blonde strands of hair behind his ears. For me, I'm happy with the haircut my Grandma gives me every few months, short and neat.

'So, you going to challenge anyone today?' Chad asks me as we slide the classroom desks across the floor to make one big communal desk in the middle of the room.

'Not sure. Unless I see a card I really want, I might just watch today. What about you?'

'Yep, I'm going to challenge Paul. I want to win back my Penrith Panthers premiership card that I lost to him yesterday.'

'You'll have to put up something big to get that back.'

'Yeah, I know.'

Chad and I finally finish setting up the classroom and after Mr Day gives us approval, we rush outside to catch the last few minutes of card flicking.

'Scott, Scott,' I hear Mitch call out as he comes running toward me with a worried look on his face. Mitch is another mate of ours. We have a small group of friends. We're close, and we're always there for one another.

'What is it, Mitch. You ok?' I ask. 'Your ... brother ... Mal,' Mitch says in between breaths. He drops both hands to his knees as he does his best to get some air back into his lungs.

'Is Mal ok?' I ask, beginning to worry.

My question is met with one of Mitch's arms as he raises one finger informing me to wait for him to catch his breath. Typical Mitch, always over-dramatic. I look at Chad as we both raise our eyebrows.

'Mal challenged Brock … and he lost,' Mitch informs me.

I look back at Chad. His face shares the same look as mine – icy shock.

'What? You serious?' I ask.

'Yep,' Mitch replies.

'What card did he lose to Brock?' Chad asks.

'Not sure, I got there just as it finished.'

'I know which card,' I say as I beeline straight towards the card flicking circle. Chad and Mitch follow.

'Which card would he use up against Brock's?' Chad asks.

'His signed Mal Meninga card,' I answer, not looking back at Chad.

'Crap!' Chad and Mitch call out at the same time as we all now beeline for the card flicking congregation.

I look over at Mal, his shoulders have slumped as he stares out toward the sports sheds, the location of his apparent defeat. Mal looks pale. As I make my way toward him, I can hear clusters of people whispering about the showdown I just missed.

Brock walks over to Mal who is stuck in the slumped position.

'Pleasure doing business with you,' he says to Mal, flashing the Mal Meninga card in front of Mal's lifeless face.

Mal can't bring himself to speak. Brock and his followers

all gloat over the Mal Meninga card, Mal's lost prized possession.

'Mal, you ok? What happened?' I ask, desperate. Mal raises his head just enough to see me. His eyes are watery. He shakes his head and doesn't say a word; he doesn't need to. I try to think of something to say. I want to be angry with him, but he is hurting, and I don't want him to hurt more.

The school bell rings to sound the end of recess. Mal's friend Grant ushers Mal toward their Year 6 classroom. I watch them as Chad does the same for me.

'Scott? Come on mate, gotta go back to class,' Chad says.

I turn to head to class, my thoughts dwell on Mal, I want to help, but what can I do?

Mal's favourite Rugby League team is the Canberra Raiders and his favourite player is Mal Meninga. Having a signed card by the immortal himself is by far one of the most famous cards getting around our school. Now it's in the hands of the enemy. I feel sorry for Mal, but that's card flicking – fun and exciting, but also cruel.

Not much was said by Mal that night at home. I tried speaking with him, but he didn't want to talk. He knew the mistake he'd made, and he knew there was no coming back from it. If only there was something I could do, I thought

The next day at school felt different. Not just for Mal and me, but with most people in the card flicking circle. I think that most of the fellow flickers saw Mal as the one who was going to finally defeat Brock and bring back a bit of hope for all who'd lost their cards to the 'Kingpin'! But Mal's losing to Brock felt like a loss for everyone.

Recess came along as it did each day. The morning was overcast and still. The card flicking circle was large as usual, but no one was flicking. Mal and his mates were nowhere to be seen. Brock was gloating as he did most days. He was flashing his new prized win, the signed Mal Meninga card. Every time he flashed the card, it made me want to lunge out and grab the card off him. But that went against the card flicking code. There were only a few rules in card flicking, and stealing a card was a big 'No'.

So now Chad and I are watching Brock as he gloats, standing among the flickers.

'Man, if only your brother beat him,' Chad says.

Brock hears Chad's comment and comes over to the both of us. 'He knew what he was getting himself into. Thinking he could beat me, hah,' Brock says with a smirky grin.

'One day someone will beat you,' I tell Brock, anger behind my voice.

'Hah, no one will beat me, not your brother, and certainly not a wimp like you,' Brock calls out as he turns back to the crowd.

'Hey, I think I might sell this crap card, anyway,' Brock calls out, holding up the signed Mal Meninga card. His followers laugh.

The anger builds up inside of me. Part of me wants to just ignore Brock and walk away, but a larger part me of me wants to challenge, challenge the 'Kingpin'.

'Oi, Brock?' I call out, Brock turns back to look at me, 'Yeah?'

'Lunchtime, I challenge you to a flick.'

'Scott, don't be stupid,' Chad pleads, pulling on my shoulder.

'What card you wanna put up against me?' Brock asks.

I reach into my shirt pocket to reveal my rare Cowabunga card. I hear people in the crowd gasp.

'OK, you're on. Your card against my New Kids on the Block card,' Brock claims.

'Nope, against the Mal Meninga card,' I say.

'No deal, I only use my New Kids on the Block card to flick.'

I think about the challenge. I hear Chad say something to me, but his words are blurred as my mind thinks quickly.

'Fine, but if I win I want the Mal Meninga card,' I yell back.

Brock takes a moment to consider the proposition. 'Deal,' he calls back, the smirking grin still on his face.

The challenge is on.

The more I think about the challenge I've foolishly laid out before myself at recess, the more the butterflies dance around in my stomach. I feel sick as I sit at my desk in the classroom. Mr Day writes some math equations on the chalkboard. I tap my school shirt pocket. I can feel my prized card sitting firmly within. The only thing that gives me some little fame at West Pymble primary school!

My best mate Chad leans over to me. 'You sure about this, Scott?'

I hear the question, but I choose not to answer. I am unsure, I feel uneasy, I want to pull out, I want to go back in time and change what I did, but I can't, not now. I have to face it, simple as that. Maybe, just maybe there will be some type of miracle. As that thought enters my mind, I hear thunder rumbling in the distance …

Chad looks at me and gives me a slow shrug of his shoulders as he continues to write down the math equation in his math book. I stare at the equation on the board. All the numbers blur into white dust that has been splashed across the black chalkboard. I swallow, the butterflies in my stomach not letting me forget what waits for me when the lunchtime bell rings.

I stare out the classroom window and see dark clouds emerging from the south of our school, the source of the thunder. A storm is approaching. We often get storms during summer, but they mainly brew up in the afternoon. It's unusual to get one around lunchtime. Perhaps the rain from the storm will save me, for today at least, I think.

I take a slow drawn-out breath as I notice Mr Day staring at me. His eyebrows screw down to meet one another as he nods his head down indicating that I should be focusing my attention on the equation and not out through the classroom window.

I look down at my exercise book on the desk, and an empty page stares back at me. What have I got myself in for?

The school bell rings, echoing through my ears and signalling my fate. I'm the last to get up from my desk. Chad waits for me at the classroom door, and I finally work up some courage to leave my desk.

'You'll be right, mate,' Chad says. There's no truth to his words and we both know it.

Chad, and I make our way to the quadrangle. A significant flock of card flickers has already emerged, eager to watch the challenge unfold. I notice others among the gathering of spectators who would not usually watch card flicking in their school breaks. More people to see me fail!

And more thunder rumbles as the dark clouds make their way closer to the school. I see Mal and his friend Grant rushing towards me, to meet me before I join the mass of card flickers.

'Scotty, what the hell do you think you're doing?' Mal asks.

'I'm trying to win back your card,' I say, nervousness distributed across my voice.

'Don't do it man,' Grant says. Mal just stares at me. He understands that there is no way for me to back out now. He knows as well as everyone else that it is against the card flicking code to back out from a challenge.

'Look, flick hard and flick fast,' Mal informs me, mimicking the flicking motion he taught me in our backyard. I nod in reply and am on my way to the circle.

'Ready to lose, wimp?' Brock asks me as I join him in the middle of the card flickers. He is wearing his sunglasses as usual and has his New Kids on the Block card gripped firmly in his hand. I can feel electricity in the air. It is still and dark as the storm clouds move directly overhead. The electricity and stillness strangely fill me with excitement and hope. I can hear parts of people's conversations: 'Cowabunga', 'Impossible', 'Mal Meninga'. I block out the conversations and try to focus.

'I'm ready ... ready to win!' displaying some confidence I don't actually feel.

'Hah, no one can beat me,' Brock claims proudly, not

bothered by my sudden reveal of coolness.

I look over at Mal. He makes a closed fist and gestures it at me. I nod.

'Winners up first,' Brock says as he takes his position to flick.

I let out a slow and long breath, trying my best to settle the nerves. Lightning flashes in the distance and is followed by growling thunder.

I look at the dark clouds above to see if a sudden downpour of rain will save me, but it feels like the heavens above are holding off until this challenge has concluded.

A few of Brock's followers call out to encourage him. Brock takes his stance, eyeing off the path ahead of him. He raises his arm as I watch on. Within a blink of an eye, Brock shoots his arm forward and releases the card from his two fingers. The card shoots through the air, spinning as it gains speed and momentum. Cheers can be heard from the crowd. Everyone knows this will be a good flick. The card travels past the central quadrangle seats, over the yellow bins, and does not lose any momentum. More lightning and thunder. Everyone's eyes are fixed on the New Kids on the Block card as it spins quickly through the air. Even the teachers on playground duty have joined in to watch the card flicking.

The card finally begins to drop as it lands perfectly on the ground, in line with the sports sheds. The landing is met with cheers. It is the longest card throw any of us have ever seen. Brock jumps in the air, not only claiming the longest flick but claiming victory. Everyone knows this is unbeatable, unless by some miracle.

I take my stance.

The dark clouds continue to rumble above. I take another long and drawn out breath to settle my nerves and focus myself for the flick of my life. Mal and my friends yell out words of encouragement. Both electricity and stillness can be felt in the air. I raise my hand, Cowabunga card firmly gripped between my two fingers. I see Brock's card sitting way off in the distance. I have to flick past it. I close my eyes and picture my flick beating Brock's.

My eyes are opened quickly by another crack of thunder. I lift my hand back behind my head. The crowd has gone silent.

This is it.

I shoot my arm forward, releasing the card from my fingers. My wrist flicks forward as fast as my arm allows. Just as the card exits my card flicking grip, an even louder snap of thunder cracks behind us, causing everyone watching to jump. The clap of thunder has released a gale force wind from nowhere. The wind blusters from behind where everyone is standing in the quadrangle. The wind howls past us all. Hair and shirts ruffle and girls' skirts are thrown up as they all work quickly to hold them down, before anyone can see under their skirts. The wind rips past everyone and takes a firm embrace of my spinning Cowabunga card.

The card accepts the force of nature behind it as it spins quickly through the air. The wind picks up pieces of rubbish as it rages across the schoolyard. Empty packets of chips and muesli bar wrappers are swept up and taken for a ride.

The card spins past the central quadrangle seats. It flies over the yellow bins. There appears to be no stopping the card as the wind takes it on an extended journey. The card jets over the New Kids on the Block card, and over the top of the sports sheds. The card finally makes a dive toward the earth and lands on the far end of the basketball court. The longest card flick imaginable, but more importantly and surprisingly to all, my card has out-flicked Brock's.

My jaw drops. Eyes wide open, a million ideas race through my mind.

'Noooo, that's not fair,' Brock cries in defeat as he falls to his knees, his voice drowned out by the cheers of everyone watching on.

I have won, I have defeated Brock!

After the challenge concluded and I had retaken ownership of the Mal Meninga card, Grant raced off to collect my card and Brock's. Brock remained in his slumped position next to me, which meant Grant was able to get his hands on the New Kids on the Block card before Brock could retrieve it. That made Grant the only known person to have held the card apart from the 'Kingpin' himself. After Grant examined the card, it was discovered that the New Kids on the Block card was secretly laminated, giving it more weight. This explained the long and consistent distance Brock had always achieved when he flicked. Word spread and everyone in the card flicking circle, especially those who had lost a card to Brock, were enraged!

The following Monday the principal's phone was ringing continuously with parents demanding their child's lost cards be returned. But, along with the fifty or so phone calls from angry parents came the ban of card flicking at West Pymble primary school.

Card flicking was no more. But it was not forgotten; nor was my achievement of defeating the undefeatable.

People even wondered if I'd controlled the weather that day. Rumours were spread and legends built.

Not least, I became a schoolyard hero.

A GIRL

Sam Herzog

PART I: No exit

I met her at her work. She was wearing a white summer dress with little green and red flowers on it. This lent her an air of lightness and frivolity. I told her that she looked good, that she looked very feminine and girly. She thought this was a bad thing and so changed into another outfit. I didn't like the new outfit, so I asked her to change back. She complied.

We left her work and headed to the sushi restaurant where we would meet the others. When we arrived, the three friends were already sitting at the table. One of them was a mutual friend of ours, a tall, fastidious boy who usually presented with a clean and precise appearance and had gone twenty-three years without ever having kissed another human being. I didn't know the other two. One of them had long, unruly hair and an absent manner which made him seem like he was on drugs (despite positively stressing later on that he was not). The other looked like a boy I had gone to school with. This boy had possessed the unfortunate character trait of being very meek. He was often bullied and eventually ended up dead the day after his twenty-second birthday after slipping over in the bathroom. I noticed his dinner doppelganger was very much alive and didn't seem particularly meek, so it seemed the similarity ended there.

The three others seemed reserved, but I wasn't. A crude joke erupted periodically from my mouth between gulps of sparkling white wine and hasty bites of a soft-shell crab. I noticed she wasn't eating much. She said that she hadn't been eating much lately, and sure enough, you could tell because she looked thinner. She didn't look thin though, just thinner. She was perfect.

After dinner, we all left the restaurant and headed to a nearby roof-top bar. When we arrived, I glanced anxiously around the roof-top, on the hunt for some 'interesting people' who, after striking up a conversation, would relay to me that they were going to a party and would ask if we wanted to come with them. ('Yes!' I would spit at them before they had even finished their sentence.) I was desperate to get away from the others (though not her, of course) who were proving to be criminally dull. Of course, it was possible that they were just excessively reserved. But in any case, it amounted to the same thing in a situation like this. I knew I was desperate to throw myself wholeheartedly into the presence of some 'very fascinating people', who would almost certainly awaken within me a new vitality; or at the very least, some sort of brief spirit of hedonism which would momentarily drown out a lurking despair.

I took a sip of my beer.

'So! What do you do?' I said, deciding to open-up a conversation with the reincarnation of my dead schoolmate.

He began to answer, and as he did so, a hot agony began to slowly accumulate within my gut. I noticed that it was nearly impossible to register anything he was saying without leaving a little deposit of irritation in my belly. Why was it so difficult to sit there and listen to him? It was as if he had never learned how to make himself seem endearing in new company, revealing certain aspects of his common, flawed human nature in the right way to elicit genuine emotion and interest in his listeners.

Further complicating this mystery was the fact that rather than evacuate this conversation or try to move it onto other pastures, I idealistically believed that he was not really a dull person – because no one is really dull, right? – and so I kept interrogating him. I thought that I just hadn't yet hit upon the right vein of precious minerals, and once I did, an iridescent ore would spill forth from his mouth and we would all be rich.

My efforts to mine him were in vain. He drawled on and on, and I kept asking him more and more questions and the whole situation was crescendoing me into a state of fever. Eventually, I decided to flee and, while sitting on a toilet seat in a dirty one-metre-by-two-metre bathroom, I attempted to contact someone (anyone) who knew of a party, or just 'anything else happening anywhere'. I messaged three people and none of them responded. I called my best friend. He told me he was busy at work and didn't know anywhere we could go. I guess I could just go home and slit my wrists, bleed out in a bathtub, I pondered to myself as I wiped my wet hands on the back of my jeans and prepared to re-join the others.

I returned from the jetliner-sized bathroom. The others mentioned that they were 'getting tired', and so our fastidious friend, as well as the one who was 'definitely not on drugs', decided to leave. This left three of us: she, I, and my previous interrogatee. A sudden thought struck me.

'What do you say we get out of here, and go to another great place I know of?' I asked. I knew this other place would almost certainly be full of 'terribly, terribly fascinating and interesting people' with youthful, red-cheeked visages in the image of Narcissus. This would provide a nice counterpoint to our current locale, which was full of what looked like puffy-faced English backpackers whom I imagined probably didn't spend much time observing their reflection.

They both nodded. As we left, I took a long look at her, carefully documenting each blonde curl which streamed down either side of her grand, green eyes. I noticed for the first time how the creamy texture of her skin intelligently offset the clear pink of her lips, and all of this was strangely soothing to me. Then it hit me that the radiant beauty which shone forth from her sa-cred features would one day fade to nothing and we were all going to die.

'Hey, I think I'm going to head off now,' the third guy said suddenly. We were stopped at a traffic-light intersection.

'Oh, uh, OK. Well it was nice meeting you, bye,' I said, distractedly.

As he disappeared across the street, I found myself being caressed by sweet strokes of relief. Now we were alone.

PART II: Everyone has their routine

Sounds of city ambience settled around us as she and I gallivanted past the old, Victorian-era terraces in the centre of the city. There were some teenagers nearby eating greasy fast food. We contemplated whether or not to start harassing them, but instead opted to fling lurid jokes at one another, each of us busting with unrestrained cackles every time a new joke was cracked.

My self-consciousness had vanished. I felt as if I didn't have a care in the world. I often felt like this when I was around her. Furthermore, we never 'made' conversation; the conversation always seemed to make itself, escaping from both of us with a natural rapidity. This I especially liked.

We arrived at the new bar. Two beautiful and elegant bartenders, a boy and a girl, sat casually conversing on a step next to the bar entrance. The boy focused on rolling his cigarette while the girl spoke precociously about matters of the highest regard (or so I fantasised). I sensed these two were prime candidates for the 'interesting and beautiful people' that I so desired; however, their physical elevation from me (the step they were sitting on was well above ground level) also reflected a psychological elevation – or so I felt – and this caused me to clam up. The en-trance to the bar was closed and so she attempted to converse with the bartenders. They glanced up at us, politely said the bar was closed, and then quickly resumed their foci, the boy on his cigarette, the girl on her one-sided conversation.

We were at a loose end. Another mutual friend of ours had

been asking us to come over to her place that night, so we now decided to meet this request by wandering over to the nearest train station. As we headed down the long escalator toward the train platform, deep in the belly of the city, I felt drunk with alcoholic honesty. I decided to put forward a certain something.

'Is there a reason that you don't want to be with me or is it that you just don't feel it?'

She looked at me. 'I dunno,' she said.

I couldn't read anything in her manner. The conversation hung there briefly for a moment, but she didn't say anything further and so I didn't ask.

We sat waiting for our train. There was something particularly ethereal about the trains that night, specifically the ones that didn't stop at the station. They would quickly glide past like fast phantoms, hardly making any noise other than a brief whooshing sound right before evaporating into thin air. Every time one flew through, I felt a tingling sensation in my neck.

The train finally arrived. I lay down across the seats with my legs over her, attempting to push a teaspoon of intimacy. She started a conversation with the two guys sitting opposite us and I started to feel anxious. One of them mentioned he was a builder. The other (not a builder) wore a black hoodie and was relatively nondescript. The builder began to talk about how he had just spent $12,000 on a pair of breast implants for his wife.

'$12,000! That's incredible!' I exclaimed.

He nodded. 'Yeah, you gotta make sure you massage 'em regularly for a while after the surgery.' We all laughed at that.

After a little while, it was our stop and so she and I got off the train. We crossed a few lonely suburban streets to our mutual friend Vicky's place. Two guys from Vicky's work were getting out of a cab. Both these guys seemed to provide the perfect foil for each other: one of them was short and chubby with a buzz cut; the other, tall and slender with mop-like hair and a thin face. We briefly exchanged pleasantries and went inside.

Vicky poured us all a drink. I gargled the 40 per cent straight liquor, hoping that it would immediately annihilate any bacteria in my mouth. For some reason, ever since childhood, I always had a fear that I had bad breath in social encounters. I always blamed this on gum and mint advertising on TV, although whether or not this was the real cause, it's hard to say. I took another sip of my drink.

'So, what do you do?' my companion for the evening asked the chubby one.

'I'm studying to become an actor,' he said.

'Really? Wow, you must be so good at accents,' she replied.

'Sure,' he said.

'But I bet you can't do a good Christopher Walken, can you?' she joked, unnecessarily touching his arm for a brief moment.

I could see that she was offering the critical extra teaspoon of attention that was necessary to have a certain desired effect. I knew what would invariably happen next: in return for this teaspoon, she would be offered a mound.

It was a routine which I can't say wasn't impressive in some way, at the very least because of its devastating effectiveness. If the Germans had ever found a way to weaponise this ability on a larger scale, I don't think it would have mattered that the Americans had the bomb.

Here's how it went: after being a little playful with him (not just him, but any him), laughing at his jokes, unnecessarily touching, what you might call 'the initial stringing up of the marionette', something would happen inside of him, some sort of transformation. First, he would hang there, dull and lifeless for a moment. Then, as though there had been flick of some switch, this marionette would spring to life, dancing, walking, and talking at her command. Then his mind would start to be corrupted by a certain objective, the pursuit of some shiny medallion which would whisper to him, telling him to come take it. Though little did he know that every time he got closer to this medallion, it would skitter ten inches back. Attempting to play this game indicated that he had already lost.

I could sense I was growing quiet. They asked me if anything was wrong.

'I'm just tired,' I said. I noticed my hand was shaking.

PART III: Stains

At some point she decided to abandon her project, asking me to come with her into Vicky's bedroom, just the two of us. One thing I should mention about Vicky was that she was extremely finicky about stains and she had even told me once that she had been diagnosed with obsessive-compulsive disorder. Funnily enough, my job at the time involved conducting research on OCD. One patient I had seen could not enter a room and turn on an appliance without having to repeatedly flick the switch on and off for an agonisingly long period of time. Another patient had been hospitalised for two years due to an intense fear of ingesting food. He was essentially afraid that if he swallowed something, the action could not then be undone. Eventually, this patient had to be fed through a nasogastric tube, until later down the track when they decided to just stick a tube straight into his stomach and feed him that way.

All of this was to say that I felt genuine empathy for Vicky, and so, when she specified that under absolutely no circumstances whatsoever could I leave any marks at all on her bed, I said to her in the most firm and assured manner, 'Look Vicky, I swear to God I won't leave any marks.'

And, you know what, after that night I now know that sometimes in life, no matter how much you mean it at the time, it doesn't matter.

After making our sacred pact, Vicky exited the room and left the two of us lying there on the bed. We started trying on Vicky's clothes. I deliberately kept choosing clothes that would show off my body or somehow make me less clothed than I needed to be. As she changed from one outfit to another, I caught glimpses of her naked body. One of my internal voices seemed to scream something at me, like a defiant brat screams at a benevolent parent. I began to grow afraid that I would suddenly lose all control and just end up taking what I desired by force.

'Look, just leave it alone, OK?' a voice in my head said.

'You're beautiful, you know,' a voice in the room said. I noticed it was my voice.

She didn't reply.

At that moment, a certain image flashed through my mind. This image was of another guy I had known, who, from what I could remember, had been taken by a girl into her room during a party. She had wanted this guy (and I assume he'd wanted her), but somehow not only did they not end up doing anything, but he also ended up parading himself around in her clothes in front of her.

I suddenly didn't want to play silly dress-ups anymore. I lay down on the bed again. This time she sat on the floor. Time passed slowly.

At some point, we both started thinking about leaving. I got up off the bed and as I went to put my hand on the window ledge to support myself, I accidently swiped at a full glass of Coca-Cola, which went flying through the air, all over the bed and down the side of the curtain.

'Jesus-Christ-goddamn-it!' I cried out.

She looked over at me. I stared back with an expression of total disbelief.

'Alright, look, we seriously have to get out of here right now before Vicky finds out,' I stated with a sense of immediate urgency.

I tried to make the stains a little less visible by rubbing them, but this didn't seem to work. She picked up her jacket and we left the bedroom. The others were dancing in the living room. I gave Vicky a hug, shook the hands of the other two, and then she and I stepped into the night.

We decided to walk to her place and watch a movie. I can't remember what we talked about on the way, but at one point, I flew feverishly into recounting a scene from a film I had seen once. The film tells the story of a man who is mistakenly accused of molesting a child. The man lives in a small town, and so when rumours spread about the accusation, he is ostracised from the community and his life naturally becomes a living hell due to this inextricable mark on his character.

During one scene in the film, a girl whom the man has been seeing finds out about the allegations. The man and the girl are in the man's house, and he states emphatically that he didn't molest the child. Then, suddenly, for a brief second, a very subtle expression flashes on the woman's face. The expression is one of doubt; she doesn't believe him, but only momentarily. Even though this expression lasts only for a second, the man is extremely offended and tells her to get the hell out, ending the relationship.

I gesticulated with extreme passion how I thought it was incredible that such a facial expression ('and only revealed for a hair's breadth of a second!') could have such powerful implications. I think I'd hoped that by telling her the story, she would think me a 'terribly passionate' individual, with such a capability for depth and profundity that she would have no choice but to resign herself to the fact that I was not someone to be taken lightly.

'But what do you think of share-bikes?' she said, as we passed a mangled, orange share-bike.

When we reached her place, I put on some of her pyjamas. Something about this didn't feel right, but I couldn't figure out what it was. We lay down in front of the TV and she put on a

Nazisploitation film that I had wanted to watch for a long time. About half-way through the film, I realised that I had no idea what was going on.

'Sorry, I'm really not following this plot at all. Why was she screaming as she ran down the hallway just now?'

I turned to her. She was looking at me with a strange expression on her face that I had never seen before. The expression flashed only for a moment, immediately wiped away like a spot of spilt coke. But then, suddenly, it was like warm saline had been injected into my heart and my whole body became relaxed and warm. This feeling rippled through me like someone had thrown a pebble into an ethereal pool of water that was my spirit.

I slowly leaned towards her and started to kiss her. At first, she was hesitant, but then the floodgates opened.

Kissing her lips was like taking a sip of water after being stranded in the desert for three days straight. As I drank her up, I stopped momentarily, moving back to take a deep look into her green eyes.

The expression on her face was that of a dead puppet. Her glass eyes had a look about them which sucked the soul right out of my chest through my gaping mouth.

I cried out. Two ants were crawling out of her left eyeball.

'Game over, fucker!' she shrieked.

I gasped and woke up.

There was daylight around me. I was lying in front of the television. There was no one around.

I lay there for a while and then I heard movement in an adjacent room. She came out and asked if I wanted to go get breakfast. After breakfast, she left to go to work.

As she was leaving, she turned to me and said, 'I'll see you soon?'.

'Sure,' I said, spotting a little ant on the ground struggling with a crumb of bread.

I quickly squashed it with my foot.

REFUGE

Matt Stuart

Day 48? Since Everything Went to Hell

Hey diary, it's been a while. I think everyone else in the city is dead. I'm not completely sure, but I think it's been bad for forty eight days. Forty eight days for everything to go from normal and the worst thing I had to handle was the commute to a crappy job, to then having no clean water, no fresh food, no phone signal. To not knowing if the four people in this minimart are the only people left alive in the world and if everyone else you know is dead. To not being able to sleep because every noise wakes you up, wired, wondering if the infected have found you.

Doug reckons there's some rural places that the army set up as disaster relief centres in the early days of the outbreak. He heard of a few places mentioned before the emergency broadcasts stopped. Tudgerah he tells us. Tudgerah is safe. If we get out of the city, everything will be okay.

Bullets left - 10

The screams followed the four of them as they plunged into the river. Even after all this time, those shrieks still chilled them deeper than the cold water.

'Fuckin' run!' Doug shouted, eyes wide.

Kate crashed along behind him, her army surplus jacket soaked by his wake. Rory howled as his injured ankle shifted against the slick stones of the riverbed. Shona grabbed his arm but Rory's weight toppled them both. Rory's cry was echoed by a terrifying chorus from those that hunted them.

'Help!' Shona cried, trying to drag Rory through the water.

Doug pitched forward onto the opposite bank, drenched and wheezing. Kate, two steps behind, stared back at the other couple. In the oncoming dusk, long screaming shadows closed in on Rory and Shona. Kate swore, unslung the .222 and aimed, squinting against the setting sun.

'C'mon!' she shouted.

The rifle barked and kicked her in the shoulder. All she could see were orange and black shadows as she braced and fired again. Fear shrivelled her gut into an icy peach stone and cut time to shreds. More screams. Frenzied splashing. The rifle pummelled her shoulder and eardrums as she fired again and again. Shona and Rory's sobs as they crawled ashore. Doug's hand on her shoulder.

'Easy, Kate. They're not crossing.'

She let out a ragged breath and lowered the rifle. The figures on the far bank paced back and forth, unable to cross running water for reasons no one had ever worked out.

'We need to get going,' Doug said, just short of giving an order. 'They'll be looking for a way across soon.'

'Give us a fucking moment, you fat prick!' Shona snapped. 'If Kate hadn't shot at those things, they'd have had us! Thanks for all your fucking help!'

Doug squatted down and checked Rory's ankle. Even in the fading light, it was clearly bent into a shape it shouldn't be. He swore and draped Rory's arm over his shoulder.

'I'm helping now, okay?'

Shona glowered and then took Rory's other arm. The injured boy hissed but managed to nod his assent to keep going.

'Kate?' Shona called back. Kate stared across the shadowed river, reloading the rifle by reflex, then broke out of her daze and followed.

Day 55? SEWH

Rory's ankle getting worse. Doug did his best to strap it but says there's only so much he can do with what we've got. Rory reckons he can keep up but we made next to no ground today. You can tell every time Doug looks at Rory, he's thinking 'dead weight'.

Shona caught one of those looks and there was a massive fight. You almost couldn't believe they're together, the way they go at each other.

I miss my phone. Only thing keeping me sane is writing in this exercise book. This and the fact we might finally get somewhere safe. Tudgerah. Supposed to be a disaster relief centre set up by the army. The only safe place we've heard about for weeks. Can't be too far away. As long as we can keep moving. I can hear Rory moan in his sleep.

Bullets left - 4

'All I'm fucking saying is, we'd be safer sticking to the riverbank instead of this bush track that looks like every man and his dog uses.'

'No,' Shona hissed back, 'all you're saying is "Let's leave Rory behind".'

She angrily sucked on the cigarette and passed it back to Doug before reaching for the roll of toilet paper. The two of them squatted back to back in the bushes off the dirt road, angrily guarding each other's backs.

'Look, I actually fucking love you, OK? If it comes down to it, I don't give a shit about Rory. I don't give a shit about Kate. You and me, babe. That's who matters.'

Shona pulled up her pants and grabbed her backpack.

'He's seventeen, arsehole. He's just a kid.'

She walked out onto the road and looked back over where they'd come from, where Rory limped along while Kate kept watch in the back. Shona waved and started back towards them.

'Shona! The toilet paper! Shona!! Fuuuuck!'

Day 59? SEWH

They got Rory.

I can't tell if those are really his screams I can hear or if it's just in my head. I think they've got our scent now.

Bullets left - 2

The screams of their pursuers rang through the trees like demented birds. They crashed through the bush in a panic.

'Stay together!' Doug choked, on the verge of throwing up.

'Keep up, babe,' Shona said as she glanced back.

She didn't see the slope that suddenly yawned in front of her. Her world tumbled into a sickening blur. She heard Doug and Kate cry out and then she came to a jarring stop. She felt pain and something wet dribbled down her forehead between her eyes. Dazed, she wiped her head and blinked at the red smear of blood on her hand. Then she realised there was something standing right in front of her. She blinked at the gun barrel aimed at her face.

'Recite the alphabet ... NOW!' Some part of her followed the barked command.

'A, B, C ...'

'She's human!'

More figures moved. She heard someone else being told to recite the alphabet. The gun barrel disappeared and she was dragged to her feet. She could see she'd fallen down onto the river bank. A large rubber boat with an outboard motor bobbed in the muddy shallows. The woman dragging her towards the boat was dressed in green, her hard face smeared with black and green paint.

'CONTACT!'

Suddenly everything moved fast again, and she was

shoved into the boat. Gunfire crackled and was answered with hideous shrieking. Shona bounced on the boat's wet deck as more soldiers leapt in, throwing Kate and Doug in with them. The outboard roared louder than the gunfire and they coasted out onto the river.

'Sound off,' a rough voice panted. There was a round of curt assents from the soldiers around them. Shona could feel the silent scrutiny of their rescuers.

'Where are you taking us?' she asked the hard faced soldier who had helped her into the boat.

'Tudgerah,' the woman replied. Cold voice. Cold eyes.

Day 64? SEWH

It's good not to be running all the time. Tudgerah is an old river town. It's been around since the gold-rush days, built on a tiny delta on the Murray and then expanding over both banks. You can see what a tourist trap Tudgerah had been before the outbreak. Gold-fossicking and four-wheel drive tours advertised in the windows of heritage-listed buildings that had been converted into cafes and antique furniture shops. Now, everyone who has survived the outbreak lives on the delta. The bridges connecting the old part of town to the mainland have been demolished by the army. Swimming or by boat is the only way in or out. So far, the infected seem to leave the place alone, though you can hear them screaming in the houses and shops across the river, and in the scrub that hugs the riverbank.

There are a few hundred locals here, and the army guys. When we were brought in, they took our rifle, and their dead-

eyed doctor checked us over for signs of infection. Doug tried to talk to him about vectors and possible lycogenic cycles, but he just ignored us and told our armed escort to initiate standard protocols. We were stripped naked, showered with high pressure hoses, scrubbed with hard brushes by faceless people in rubber suits. After, we were given back everything that wasn't a weapon or our clothes.

Hugh, a local who'd been regional co-ordinator for the SES when everything went to hell, explained it to us, doing his best to retain his dignity before our disbelief. Standard protocol is that everyone here except the soldiers wears nothing but a clear vinyl jumpsuit, so no-one can hide signs of infection.

Standard protocol. He must have said that a hundred times, holding out the jumpsuits to us imploringly. One of the soldiers nearby growled at us from behind a gas mask to put them on or get kicked back outside. That was what got us to go along in the end. Then we were cleared to stay.

Every time I walk, the clear plastic suit crinkles and bunches and mists with sweat. It's every dream I've ever had about being naked in public, just magnified by a thousand. Everyone in Tudgerah except the soldiers wear the same suits we do, but they seem to have gotten used to it. Gazes that are barely friendly constantly crawl over me. I feel like everything about me is laid bare. I'm relieved when looks take me in and then dart away. I try to ignore the ones that linger. We get given mandatory work assignments in a couple of days. It's good to not be running all the time.

No such thing as privacy

'What the fuck are you looking at, mate?' The soldier smirked at Shona's anger.

'Settle down, love,' he drawled. Shona's outburst of swearing brought every eye on the scene. She didn't seem to notice the attention.

'Every time I walk past, I've got you ogling me like a piece of meat. And if it's not me, it's her,' Shona jerked a thumb at Kate who was still carrying her half of the water collected from the rainwater catchments.

'Can't blame a guy for having a look,' he replied and the smirk turned into a scowl.

'Are you fucking kidding me? We're actual people, you dickhead! Dressed to the standard your shitty little society here set out. Treat us with a bit of bloody respect and apologise.' The gathered crowd was silent. Shona's burning gaze swept her audience.

'Apologise,' she repeated, more loudly.

Hugh pushed himself through the crowd. His constant perspiration gave his balding head a slick crown, and a merciful misted veil on the inside of his suit.

'Now see here, Shona, you can't talk like that. This man risks his life every day to keep us safe.' The crowd murmured in agreement.

'If you don't like it here, maybe you should just leave,' someone shouted. Shona's eyes were wide with disbelief.

'You think I want to be stuck in here? You think this is what I want?' The murmurs around her turned into angry shouts.

'Maybe if you'd fought a bit harder instead of whinging, you'd still have a place of your own to call home!'

'The more people we bring in, the more risk we bring to ourselves from those things outside!'

'Didn't see you complaining when we pulled you off that riverbank, love,' the soldier said, his smile back with full effect.

'Oh, fuck this!' Shona shouted.

Day 70? SEWH

Shona's gone.

She woke me up, told me she was going. Told me she'd stolen some supplies from storage. Told me the boats were too well guarded and that she was going to swim for it, then hugged me and told me to take care. I asked where Doug was. She had laughed and her eyes got angry and wet. No matter how scared she was, she didn't ask me to come with her. I guess another rejection might have broken the courage she'd summoned to leave.

I sat here waiting, expecting to hear a shout or gunshots, or anything. I think she's done it. I think everyone is looking for things breaking in, not out. But I think being alone, Shona is going to be in trouble.

And I think I know where they're keeping my rifle.

Bullets left - 2

They had a tearful, shivering reunion on the banks of the river outside Tudgerah. Shona hugged Kate tight, and whispered a score of fierce thank-you's into her ear. Kate had seen a boat shed not far upstream in her time hauling water. She was sure she'd seen boats moored there. The two of them stuck as close to the bank as they could, but eventually had to move inland. The river current was too cold and too strong for them to swim.

Moonlight through foliage dressed them in silver-black lace as they crept through the bush. For what felt like hours, they never spoke a word, never made a sound, never let go of each other's hand. Then they saw the plasterboard boat-shed, white as bone through the trees. Everything was still and suddenly Kate's skin crawled. The shadows around them shifted and something wheezed in the dark. They broke hands and bolted.

The shadows screamed and flailed after them. Kate saw shadows in the boatshed squirm with a parody of life and she staggered to change course, heading instead for the boats she saw tied up on the small pier. Shona wailed behind her. Kate turned and saw them on her. Red lines opened on Shona in the moonlight. Kate unshouldered and fired in panic. Shona's head jerked and her wailing ceased.

Hot vomit burned in Kate's mouth and she turned and ran for a boat, some part of her brain locked on the moment of the rifle's kick and Shona's final clonic twitch. Instinct took over and Kate dived into an aluminium boat, frenziedly unmooring it. Her hands ripped open and bled but she didn't notice. The boat freed, she kicked savagely at the pier and scrambled for the outboard motor.

She was almost thrown into the water as a screaming horror leapt into the boat. It bore her down, its stinking palm ground into her face and kept her pinned. Its brown teeth clicked together as it snapped at her throat. Her panicked hand found the trigger of the rifle and snatched at it. The rifle writhed between their bodies like a snake. The muzzle flash blotted out her vision. Agony set her face on fire. The thing above her spasmed and fell into the water.

She stared up at the stars, trying to see them past the ones that danced madly across her vision. She felt numb to everything, even the burning pain in her face. The current took her small boat and dragged it back to Tudgerah.

Day ??

First time I've felt like I can focus enough to write. Not much light in here. Whenever the dead-eyed doctor comes to check up on me, his torch is blinding. He told me I'm quarantined. I've told him I'm not infected. I was covered in that thing's blood but it didn't bite me. He doesn't seem inclined to take chances. I've given up asking how long I'll be down here.

Oh god, Shona, I'm so sorry. Mum and Dad, I miss you and I love you so much. And it hurts so much that we never got the chance to say goodbye.

I'm so cold. I feel like all I've done is drink my fill to bursting from some subterranean lake, and now I'm full of cold darkness. I miss my phone. I miss being connected to ev-

eryone. Anyone. If I didn't have this book I'd go insane.

Bullets left - 0

'What's she doing in there?' The soldier glanced through the bars of the cell at the crouched pale figure in the gloom.

'Diary, I think. The bloke that came in with her brought it down and left it here for her.'

The doctor scowled. 'That's a violation of hazardous items protocol, you idiot. Confiscate it and have it put in the archives with the others.'

'Do you want to look it over before I do?'

The doctor stared at the soldier.

The soldier looked away, thinking he'd make his own decision on what to do. 'Right. Sorry, sir.'

MARA IMMACULATA

Marjorie Banks

Jewels of coloured light illuminated the ancient grey flagstones as morning sun flooded through the stained glass.

Mara stood by the altar for a moment, the cobalt and crimson of a saint's robe cast over her feet. It was a quiet time of day, a time when she rarely encountered anyone else except the priest.

For many years it had been a near-daily pilgrimage for her to visit the church at this hour. Over that time any faith she had once imagined had fallen away. She came for the silence and communion with the ancients.

The ancients who had carved their pagan traditions into this building. They had woven a defence of stone garlands, arcane symbols and demons to keep out any newer god from some foreign desert land. And so the church stood: empty and hollow, sacred to forces more primaeval, forces of the forest, the storm, the river, the mountain crags.

'Good morning.' The priest raised a hand to Mara as he went about his business.

He knows, she thought. We share the same knowledge, that there is nothing here. He had the face of a saint himself, and though his hair was grey and his face lined, sometimes she saw the ghost of the younger man in him. The sacrifices, too, that the younger man had made.

It was then she felt the first twinge, the first odd dizziness. The first warning of the fragility of her body, its vulnerability. She sat down on a pew and momentarily closed her eyes, glad the priest had passed by. Glad that he would not witness her sudden weakness, and embarrass her with any expression of concern or offer of assistance.

The jewels of light still scattered over her. A gargoyle, adorned in marble ivy, leered from on high.

Mara lived a solitary life but not a lonely one. She had worked for many years as a legal secretary, flawlessly efficient, reliable and discreet. She was indifferent to the work; after the decades it washed over her. Had she had any ambition she might easily have taken articles herself. Over time she had come to know most areas of law as well as any qualified solicitor.

But she was content to continue as she did. A small legacy had enabled her to retire early, just before her fiftieth birthday, and retire she did. The senior partners entreated her to stay, but she was resolved to leave.

It meant no real change to her life, other than the weekend now stretched across the week. Were it not for the Sunday bells, there was little to mark the passage of time. She might read more, she thought, or take up some artistic pursuit. She had sketched well, as a girl.

It was also natural, at this age, that there would be other changes. Mara had anticipated such a thing for some years, but when the cessation came, it was not quite as she had expected. She had taken and studied brochures from the doctor's surgery, and knew that there were medications one could take if required. With side-effects, of course, but that was always the way.

She had never married nor thought much of marriage, so the closing of this door did not seem unduly distressing.

Only as the months passed, she became uneasy. A little less bread and butter, and giving up the sugar in her tea, had not quite offset the tightening of her waistband. She had wavered over whether to let out a couple of skirts or perhaps try a more rigorous regime. She recalled her grandmother and her aunts: rigid-backed, rail-thin women from middle age until the day they died. Mara's mother had died before this time of life, so she could not compare her experience.

Brisk walking, perhaps? There were notices pinned up at the local community centre advertising exercise classes and keep-fit clubs, but Mara did not feel inclined towards any of these.

Time passed, and she still did not feel well. Weakness frequently overcame her limbs, and she felt nausea often. To retire and fall ill the same year was a bitter blow, if, as she feared, it was something serious.

In the end she went to the doctor, who frowned a little as he examined her. 'You say you had your fiftieth birthday in May?' he asked, Mara nodded in response. 'Such an event is not unheard of, at your age, though rare perhaps.'

Rare? At forty, perhaps, Mara thought, but hardly at fifty.

'Really quite rare indeed,' the doctor continued, deepening his patient's confusion.

She began to understand what he meant, and a heavy resignation filled her. Perhaps she had always known. From that first time when the dizziness had overcome her. A way of life was ending. An independence. If she had valued anything at all, it was her independence.

Now, her methodical mind began to plan. She was not morbid, but preferred to be prepared. There would be a course of treatment, perhaps, and nurses. At some point the local hospice. Somehow she must bear the intrusion. The reliance on others.

This vision absorbed her, and she did not clearly hear the rest of what the doctor was saying, until he mentioned booking in at the hospital for a scan.

'Of course,' she said, and still in her future world, she took the sheaf of documents he gave her, and left the surgery.

She went to the church, for where else could she go? She was not ready to bring her thoughts into her own home. To pollute it with the agony of the disruption that awaited her.

The priest was there, and he smiled and nodded at her. He did not remark on her coming at such an uncustomary time.

Mara sat by the altar once again. The light had moved to the west by now, and no jewels fell upon her. A passer-by might have assumed she was praying, but she was thinking.

If she could become stone …

To have the stone vines gradually grow around her, twisting up past her feet, up her body, encircling her. Binding her to the carved stone of the pillar. All would be still, all silent. There would be no more pain. If she had ever felt a bitter envy towards anything, she felt it now. Towards the angels and other creatures adorning the transept: fixed there in eternal peace. Too high to be disturbed, too cold to feel. Motionless. Inviolate.

She drifted through the next week. Almost wondering whether it was worth it, she made her way to the hospital and was directed to the radiology department. Mara found the sympathetic manner of the female doctor and nurses oddly bright.

'All seems to be in order, Mrs Bennett.'

'Miss Bennett,' Mara corrected, disliking the heartiness of the other woman's tone.

The doctor looked briefly disconcerted, but recovered. 'My apologies, but it's been written on your papers incorrectly. Nothing wrong with keeping your maiden name these days.'

'I'm not married,' Mara said.

'Or that either,' the doctor continued quickly. 'Quite the norm these days. Just so long as everyone's healthy, isn't that right?'

For the first time in a dark week, a small flame of hope flickered within Mara. Until this moment, she had not realised how much she minded about the inevitability of it all. Suddenly there was a glimpse of a golden vista. Entirely new possibilities. She was being given years, decades, perhaps. All the things she could now do, that she had never done nor even thought about wanting to do. 'Do you mean you have good news?'

'I should say so. Of course there are more tests we can do, and some of the older patients we see prefer that, for peace of mind. But based on what I'm seeing today, it all looks very healthy. We'll see you again in two weeks. Just keep doing what you're doing, and try to relax.'

A new weakness washed over Mara. This time of relief.

For the first time since her original appointment she found herself able to glance at the medical notes. A phrase struck her. 'Geriatric primigravida'. She felt affronted at this. Retired she may be, with a half century under her belt, but she hardly felt geriatric.

The doctor saw her frowning. 'Is something wrong, Miss Bennett?'

'Geriatric is rather a … damning term.'

The doctor smiled. 'Rather unflattering, isn't it? I'm sorry the profession hasn't found something more tactful. If it's any consolation, it's used for anyone over the age of thirty-five.'

'Thirty-five?' Half of one's three-score-years-and-ten, Mara thought.

'Given the average age for a first time pregnancy is now over thirty, it's probably time the terminology got an overhaul,' the doctor continued.

Mara was silent for a moment. 'Pregnancy?'

'Yes. The risks obviously do go up with age, but from what I've seen today, it's all looking very positive.'

She had the wrong notes, Mara thought. The wrong patient. 'I think you must be mistaken,' she said.

Now the doctor frowned. 'Mistaken?'

Once more sitting in the church, her stone friends surrounding her, securing her, everything quiet and safe and unchanged, Mara replayed in her mind the rest of the conversation.

'I'm not married, doctor.'

'You don't need to be married!'

'What I mean to say is, that I don't have a gentleman companion of any kind.'

'I'm afraid it doesn't necessarily require a regular partner, Miss Bennett. Just once is enough.'

But Mara had never had a gentleman companion. Such a thing had been no more to her taste than marriage. She found herself unable to articulate this. It had been very awkward. The doctor had thought her deluded, an old maid in denial. You couldn't rely on menopause, the doctor had said. She'd seen a dozen or more 'change of life' conceptions in her time. It only took the one encounter. The one slip-up. The one risk, and a prayer that didn't get answered.

Mara had left, in more of a daze than when she had arrived. She was back in her sanctuary now. Back in the cool, the hollow silence. The empty altar, derelict of a deity.

It was cancer, she knew it must be. The doctor was mistaken. These mix-ups happened.

On the wooden pew, she gazed up at the stained glass, her hand resting on her stomach. How long did she have to live? Was there any point letting out her skirts, or would a safety pin suffice? Her mother had died of a stomach tumour. It had not been a long process, from the diagnosis until the end. She had suffered, though. Mara could only hope to face her trial with the same courage.

The priest approached her from the nave. The sun, then shining from the south west, formed a halo behind his head.

He came to her, and Mara found she was not surprised when he knelt before her, his head lowered as in prayer. He looked up at her, the reverence of the saints in his eyes. Grey eyes, like the statues and the stone.

And then he spoke.

'In my youth I was given a vision. Due to it, I made a pilgrimage, and it brought me here. Throughout these past years I have waited, and I have doubted everything. I have doubted my vows, my order, the church. I have doubted God – all the gods created by humankind. All of them are as dust to me.'

His eyes regarded the church, the altar, the jewelled glass of the windows. For a moment Mara saw it all as dust: crumbled into ruins a thousand years hence, the sun beating down on a green land dried to desert.

'Except for my vision,' the priest continued. 'All my life, it has been the one thing I could not doubt. The one thing I held fast to. I knew not in what form it would come, but I knew that it must come to pass. And last night the signs came to me for the final time.'

He bowed his head again.

'All blessings upon you, and through you all things are blessed, from the dawn of the first sun until the dusts of the end of time.'

A SKYFUL OF STARS
Sharon Dean

*'People do not consist of memory alone. People have feelings,
imagination, drive, will and moral being.'*
Donna Cohen & Carl Eisdorfer (geriatric mental health specialists)

When I find Norma, she's sitting on a couch in the lounge area with several other residents. A few are asleep in their chairs, most are watching TV. But Norma is staring into the distance, a half-smile playing on her face. She's wearing a brooch I haven't seen before – an Art Deco piece set with black onyx and fragments of marcasite. Perhaps one of her daughters dropped in earlier today?

'Hi Norma,' I say, crouching so my face is level with hers, 'I like your brooch.'

Norma turns in the direction of my voice and her smile broadens. I take this as a cue to sit beside her. The couches here aren't the type you sink into with a happy sigh, but I feel comfy. Having been on my feet all day, I'm tempted to simply close my eyes and soak up the companionable atmosphere. After all, I'm on a lunch break, it's not like I'd be skiving off.

But in my hands I feel the weight of a book I've brought with me. Printed in landscape format, it's so large that when I turn back the cover the pages extend across both our laps.

Norma looks down at the lines of text, still smiling.

'You wrote the beautiful poems in this book,' I tell her. 'I'll read a few.'

Not long after starting my job at a large aged care centre on the far north coast of NSW, I ran into a neighbour, the poet Quendryth Young, who said she often visited the facility's high-level dementia-care unit. One of her friends lived there: a former teacher and writer by the name of Norma Balzer.

'Norma and I met twenty years ago,' Quendy explained. 'We often wrote together. With another writer we published a collection of poetry called *My Day's Circle*. Then Norma wrote her own book, *Once Upon a Farm*.'

As a member of the aged care centre's activities staff, I was mostly rostered on in the dementia-care units, where I organised singalongs and art therapy sessions. I'd met Norma, and wasn't surprised to hear she was a published poet. Although I'd never shared a logical conversation with her, I'd noticed she had an intriguing vocabulary and carried herself with the bearing of a woman with deep intellect and compassion. Anyone watching her out of earshot would get the impression she was making a high degree of sense.

And maybe she was – in another dimension, in her own private world.

Quendy loaned me a copy of *Once Upon a Farm*, and I immersed myself in descriptions of life on the Dunoon dairy farm where Norma had raised six children with her husband while completing a teaching degree, working as a librarian, and writing a novel for young adults.

Reading Norma's poems, I enjoyed her observations of the simple wonders of the natural world, whether she was admiring *four parrots in a flash of flight,* or an old white horse that was *bony-rumped and grubby-hocked/but white-washed in the light of moon.*

I soon discovered, however, that threaded through poems about the *busy, multi-coloured cloth/of farming life* were mindful musings on the ageing process. Describing a visit to a nursing home, the poet wondered:

Who are these people?
Who have they been?
Before they were here ...
in Limbo,
waiting
to die ...
completely.

Another poem, a meditation on being drugged for a medical procedure in 1990, revealed the poet's fear of losing her mind.

The question all the time
is What's my mind?

and why I care.
I lost it for a while
last time.
It wasn't there.

In that other world
I coped
with callers at my door
(who really weren't).

I dealt with them as need arose
with social skills
acquired in life.

I knew myself
as actor in the play –
Real, no more than they.

And in the end,
I coped
I came back
me.

But kept a healthy nervousness
of being altogether free.

Knowing that Norma was today living with some severe symptoms of dementia – memory loss, disorientation in place and time, and problems with reasoning and abstract thinking – made the experience of reading such lines all the more poignant. Before long, I began asking myself similar questions to those posed about the old people in her poems: *Who is this person? Who has she been?* But then I moved on to pondering: *Who is she now? And what makes her happy?*

During the short time I'd worked in aged care, I'd discovered that dementia-care service providers like to measure things: dinners served, pills dispensed, rooms occupied. Sitting with Norma's book, I mentally listed a few oversights: acts of kindness, creative collaborations, new friendships.

Every day I was learning that people living with dementia retain interests they enjoyed before their memory loss. Fortunately, Norma's poetry contained plenty of clues about things that made her soul sing. There was *the smell of paddock at the end of a town day*, the poetry of TS Eliot, and even the ordinary experience of sitting in the sun with a cup of tea while listening to birds and watching *the gentle flap of sheets on the clothesline*. Overall, the thing Norma most wanted, her writing spelt out, was to *live this moment as it is*.

Norma had spent years reading and writing poetry. Perhaps now I could read some of her poems aloud to her?

So here I am, a few days later, walking through the high-level dementia-care unit in search of Norma. She's not in her bedroom, so I'll look elsewhere. As I head down an empty corridor, I recall reading about the American writer Ralph Waldo Emerson, who in his early seventies developed a slow, progressive memory disorder that ravaged his concentration and short-term memory, dulling his perceptions to the point where he could no longer follow a conversation or understand what he was reading.

According to Emerson's biographer, Phillips Russell, the great writer's daughter entered her father's study one day and found him 'reading very intently in one of his own books'. Aware that the book would have possessed for her father 'a novelty … exactly like he would have found in the work of an unknown author', the young woman was bemused when he looked up at her and exclaimed, 'Why, these things are really very good.'

I can't help wondering if Norma, on hearing her poems, will react in a similar way.

Once I've located Norma amid the sleepyheads in the TV lounge, I start with a poem called 'Gaia Experience'. It's about the tidal pools at Broken Head.

How do I tell of crab
the way it ought to be –
Plump, sweet, white,
And washed in sea –
But textured … how?
No word!

I look at Norma in surprise – *No word!* – and raise my

eyebrows even higher when she mimics my astonished expression.

The language lets me down.

'Yes,' Norma says. 'They'll be coming around soon. And it really is a problem that those pictures haven't come down.'

Its coral, crusted shell,
crushed,
and spiralling
to find the moray eel,
pool bound.

'Bound,' Norma agrees. 'One day it's going to tip over completely.'

How do I tell of feet,
their separate ecstasy,
in iced, salt swirl of tide
through wet, black rock,
froth-trailed!

I look again at Norma, who fulfills her part in what is becoming an intimate and collaborative performance by offering me several more free-flowing sentences.

Amphibian I,
precariously
in niche on rock
feet free
in ice, arms and face
in burn of sun
and wind in hair.
I celebrate the strength
of muscle-play
with rush and suck of sea
that hold me –
mollusc –
here.

Norma again responds in a manner that strikes me as a liberating and sublimely irrational form of free association. We're playing with language. On the surface, nothing she says makes sense, but the underlying current of emotion feels real and enlivening, like a spontaneous dialogue between Norma and her published poems, as well as a playful conversation between friends who are making up the rules as they go.

I release any expectation that Norma will recognise the poems as her own. She is listening to me read as though each line is completely fresh, nodding encouragingly, and seeming to revel in the beautiful rhythms of language that washes over us.

Eventually, I turn to three short stanzas called 'Proverb – (after the Chinese)'. The stanzas resemble haiku, in that each is comprised of three short lines. I read the first two lines of the first stanza …

Once a day
Walk barefoot …

… and am about to progress to the third line, when Norma pipes up: 'In the morning grass.'

We look at each other and grin. Norma has delivered the final line of the first stanza, exactly as it appears on the page. Her expression seems to be saying, 'Now where did that line come bubbling up from? Isn't life a mystery!'

With growing excitement, I read the first two lines of the second stanza …

As often as you may,
Stand alone …

… to which Norma responds: 'In a skyful of stars.'

She's done it again. 'Beautiful!' I say, repeating the line a couple of times before moving onto the third and final stanza.

And once in a while,
Walk ...

But Norma begins free-associating again, and entertains us both with several new, alternative lines for the final stanza. When she's finished her contribution, I read the published version ...

And once in a while,
Walk
In a crowded street

'A mad street,' Norma suggests. 'A mad street in the crowded room.'

'Yep, a mad street,' I nod, and we sit there together on the couch in the aged care centre, exhilarated and content.

According to psychotherapist Sharon Snir, communicating with someone with dementia is very different from the way we communicate with others. 'Most of their understanding does not come from what is being said but how we say it,' she writes. 'Body language, attitude, eye contact, tone of voice, touch, acknowledgement, warmth and kindness all contribute to good communication.'

As I get up to leave, I have no doubt that Norma's poetry has enabled us to enjoy a warm and genuine connection.

Quite fittingly, it was Ralph Waldo Emerson who noted that, 'for everything you have missed, you have gained something else'. As this line pops into my mind, I realise that whatever my dialogue with Norma lacked in terms of intrinsic meaning or logic, it made up for in terms of openness, vitality and sheer creative joy.

I want to tell Norma that I'll return with more poetry tomorrow – perhaps something by TS Eliot, or maybe even a verse or two from her close friend Quendy– but decide instead to simply squeeze her hand.

As I move towards the door, however, it's Norma who provides a touching and poetic farewell. 'Next time,' she announces, 'you can sit on my veranda and watch my sky.'

VENGEANCE AND BETRAYAL

Grace Lightly

They had been in a relationship for three and half years, had trudged through the furrows and sailed the crests of love like most other couples. Now, their relationship was on an all-time high. The sex was only getting better and their effortless rapport and mutual admiration were obvious to everyone.

Philip recently turned sixty. With hair combed over a bald patch and a steadily growing paunch, he had survived two failed marriages. Baggage cropped up now and then, triggered by unhappy memories, but for a while things had been going smoothly.

Rachel was fifty-two but looked much younger. She was fit and slim with hazel eyes and raven black hair with a monthly colour. Although the widow of a man many years her senior, she had had a happy marriage, based on mutual trust, honesty and respect.

Philip and Rachel were a liberal-minded couple. They agreed on an 'open' relationship with occasional casual encounters on the side, if both parties agreed. Their guiding principle was 'our relationship is paramount' and they couldn't do anything that might hurt the other party. Outside encounters were meant to enhance their bond but if either felt it could have a negative impact, the contact would be rejected.

Philip and Rachel had both dated other people when they went through a temporary break-up earlier on. When they got back together again, Philip insisted that Rachel continue seeing her young lover. There was no threat from a casual, no-strings-attached arrangement, he thought.

Rachel however, was willing to give up her younger lover.

'I've always been a serial monogamist,' she told Philip. She felt ambivalent. Why retain the young lover when Philip more than satisfied her needs in every respect? But Philip insisted she keep seeing the young one, so she did. Maybe he got illicit pleasure from thinking about them together.

Philip met a few women on a dating site and discussed them with Rachel. 'Ultimately, it feels unsatisfying … meaningless,' he declared, and said he'd stopped seeing them. Rachel never thought to question it further.

They lived a few blocks apart and both worked from home. One afternoon mid-week, Philip popped over to see Rachel. It was clear her lover had just left.

'I've been meaning to tell you,' Philip said, 'I've actually been seeing someone for the past few months.'

Rachel blanched. Her mouth went dry then the words all tumbled out at once.

'I thought we agreed to discuss outside activities to see if it was working for us? I thought the whole idea was transparency? You knew about my guy ... you encouraged me to keep seeing him even when I said I wanted to stop!' She checked her rising pitch as she struggled to stay calm. 'How can I say how I feel if I don't know what's going on?'

'I know,' Philip replied, averting his gaze and staring out the window. 'I should have told you a long time ago but the longer I left it, the harder it became.' He looked back at her. 'It was never the right moment and I was afraid of your reaction.' Red blotches were spreading across his face and neck.

'Why would I say no to you when you said yes to me? I believe in fair play. And you, crusader of egalitarian policies and champion of women's rights who abhors the double standard! Wouldn't you find that somewhat hypocritical?'

Philip flinched, wondering if he'd done the right thing to tell her. 'This is just what I was worried about,' he replied in a self-justifying tone. 'In theory you say you'd accept it but in practice, it's very different.'

'You can't know what my reaction would be unless you tell me.' Rachel felt her body shaking with rage and on the verge of tears. Her lip quivered.

'True ... I was a coward,' he said, head drooping from shame and too many hours spent straining over a screen. 'I should have told you sooner.'

'How often did you see her?' Rachel sat on the bed, propped up with pillows. 'Did you tell her about me?' Now she wanted as much information as she could get. Not wanting him to clam up, she tried not to sound angry or hurt.

'I saw her about five or six times.'

'So about once a month,' Rachel interjected, making note

of the information for future reference.

'Yeah, I guess. I told her I was in an open relationship but wasn't leaving my girlfriend.'

'Open!' Rachel flung her hands into the air as her voice crescendoed. 'Please explain how "open" means you tell her about me, but don't tell me about her! So it's OK to deceive me, the woman you claim to be the love of your life, your first priority?' Rachel's nostrils flared and her breathing was rapid.

Philip was floundering, the panic rising in his voice. 'When she asked me if I was in love with you, I told her "Yes, very much so". I also said "no weekends", that it was just a casual thing.' He felt himself sinking deeper into irredeemable territory.

'So that makes it OK?' Rachel's eyes narrowed into slits but she kept quiet, fuming silently.

Philip jabbered on, telling Rachel how the last time he'd slept with Tammy, she mentioned that she'd never been with a woman but wanted to try.

How tacky and pathetic, Rachel thought, to convey that information while fessing up to his clandestine affair.

'Did you think I'd be interested?' Rachel's thoughts whirled ahead of her words. It was meant to be rhetorical but Philip dug his grave deeper with each reply.

'No, no. When she asked me about bringing you into it, I said I didn't think it'd be a good idea.'

'Well, yes, after this sudden revelation. But who knows? If you'd told me about her then, we might have had a three-way.'

It wasn't the sex that bothered Rachel; it was the breach

of trust. What was acceptable for her applied to him but she said nothing more. She wanted him to feel he'd done the right thing by finally speaking up.

Later that day, on Facebook, she posted, 'Paradise is an illusion and all men are liars'.

Philip, having unburdened himself, went home feeling lighter, relieved of the self-inflicted torment and guilt he'd been carrying around for five months by keeping his fling a secret. Pleased with their civilised discussion, he emailed Rachel.

'I have sent you a copy of Tammy's profile on RSVP,' proving his commitment to revealing everything.

And that's when it hit her – how to extract her revenge.

She would go online and create a fake profile. One that Philip, if he was still visiting the site, would never recognise as Rachel. It would be done with one guiding principle. Nothing was to be the truth.

She looked up Tammy's profile and saw a petite, classy-looking Asian woman with a hint of coquettishness. Rachel could tell from the spelling and grammar that her English was limited. It said she was after a serious relationship, waiting for someone who could 'look after her'.

Rachel glanced at the requests for contact. She should have chosen: 'I'd like to get to know you. Would you be interested?' or 'Your profile caught my eye so I thought I'd say hi!' but she was in a hurry to move things along so she chose:

'I feel we could really hit it off and have fun. Do you want to explore things further?'

'Explore.' That was the hook. Philip had used the word

when justifying outside relationships, 'We can explore, experience, push the boundaries.'

That night she checked her inbox.

'Yes,' she shouted, punching her fist in the air. 'Bingo!'

Tammy had taken the bait. Now she would be the lure for Rachel to snare her prey.

'Love you long-time,' Rachel sneered into the screen, 'love you just long enough'.

'Grace' was Rachel's nom-de-plume. She liked the irony of it. She said she liked wine although she never drank, and said she was Australian when she was from Eastern Europe. When she wrote 'looking for men or women,' there was nothing in the profile that Philip or anyone else could identify. Few were privy to the sexual exploits of her younger days.

Rachel suggested to Tammy that they meet for drinks. Tammy invited her back to her place for green tea, and it was on. 'Grace' hadn't been with a woman for many years and was pleased it felt natural and spontaneous. Tammy delighted in her company and in discovering a new arena of sensual pleasures. They met every Tuesday for several weeks at Tammy's little studio above a printing lab in San Souci.

After a few visits, Rachel began gleaning information after they made love. Had she had much luck on the site, met any interesting men?

Gradually, Tammy told Rachel about Philip, how he was in an 'open' relationship but loved his girlfriend and wasn't planning to leave her. Rachel listened, as she stroked Tammy's silky skin. Rachel had nothing against Tammy. It was Philip she wanted to punish for deceiving her.

Tammy had told Philip she'd never been with a woman and asked him about his girlfriend. He thought it wasn't a good idea so they left it at that. Rachel had been waiting for this chance.

'Well,' she said, coyly, 'do you want to try with me and him?'

Tammy's eyes gleamed. 'I was shy to ask. It's OK with you?'

'I don't know. Do you think I'll like him?' Rachel said, quickly adding, 'I suppose if you like him, I will too. How about Friday night? Will you let him know?'

Rachel played out each likely scenario in her head then decided to take it a step further. Her personal humiliation would be his public undoing. Rachel contacted an old friend who was a criminal barrister. She said she was writing a story and, wanting to make it sound authentic, wanted to know how people planted drugs and what the process would be if police were called to the scene.

On Friday night, thunder clapped and lightning lit the sky with jagged flares. Rachel parked her car well out of sight. Heavy raindrops pelted down on her as she pulled her hood over her head and made a dash for Tammy's place. Arriving early, Rachel asked to use the bathroom. On the way, she slipped into the bedroom while Tammy was preparing drinks and Asian snacks inside her tidy little kitchen. Rachel took a latex glove from her pocket, slipped it on then took out a little bag of white powder. Quietly, she pulled the underwear drawer open and dropped the little bag in.

The doorbell rang. Rachel held her breath from behind

the door as she tried to overhear the conversation.

'Rachel, come. I want introduce you,' Tammy called from the living area.

Rachel swaggered into the room, looking down at the floor, her opening line rehearsed and ready as she raised her eyes to meet the man standing there.

'This is Frank,' Tammy said. 'Frank meet Rachel.'

Rachel's mouth dropped open but no sound emerged. 'How do you do?' she managed to stammer. She grabbed Tammy by the arm, saying, 'Excuse us a moment,' and dragged her into the kitchen.

'Who is he?' she seethed through gritted teeth. 'You told me 'Philip' was coming. You didn't tell me anything about this guy?'

'Philip ring two hour ago,' Tammy whimpered, bewildered by Rachel's response. 'He say he can't come. Can't see me no more. I don't want spoil tonight so ring other man I meet on RSVP. I tried ring you, but your phone turned off.'

Rachel flew into the bedroom, shoved the powder in her pocket and strode back into the living room. 'Look, Frank, I'm sure you're a very nice bloke and all but I was expecting someone else.' She grabbed her bag and slammed the front door behind her.

Down in the street she took out her phone which had been on silent. A message with the number of the Narcotics Department was on the screen and there was one missed call.

It was from Philip.

CYNTHIA'S LAST FOXTROT

Richard Hambleton

'I might be an old duck,' Cynthia said, flipping a clutch of legal documents onto the table, 'but I'm not a turkey.' She smiled at Stella, who cackled at the joke, sipping her tea.

Lines of mirth cracked Stella's cheeks. There was the same sublime glint in her eyes that Cynthia remembered from, oh gosh, way back in high school. And for a moment came that familiar, refreshing, mellow peace that settled between them, a feeling that had nourished and protected the friends for all those years. They smiled together in silence. Then Cynthia leaned across and kissed her dear friend on the cheek.

'My dear Stella,' she said, 'you and me, we'll be alright. We'll be together here in this house, forever.'

And Stella's face lit up as she looked Cynthia in the eyes, smiled, and mouthed the word 'for-ever'.

Cynthia snapped into business, shuffling the documents into a neat pile.

'Bring on the sharks,' she said and they laughed together, that old familiar concoction of throat chuckles and nasal snorts. And from the world outside came the creak of an ancient iron gate, a long familiar note, slow and sad, full of rust and memories.

Cynthia looked up at the sound and glanced at Stella.

'That used to be my husband coming home,' she said. 'Today it will be that evil prick who wants to build town houses over my dead body. He's a greasy bastard. Kevin's body was hardly cold when he landed like a vulture.'

Through a split in the drapery Cynthia watched the long yellow car as it crackled up the gravel drive between the marbles, the cherubs, satyrs and serpent-encrusted birdbaths, and then she closed the tall velvet drapes that were like cinema curtains, turning to Stella, cup of tea wobbling in one hand.

'A fucking yellow Bentley, Stel, wouldn't you know? Yellow. You wouldn't think they'd be allowed to paint a Bentley yellow. Fucking American market. Anyway, sit there, Stel. I'll go and get him. Don't say anything. Just let me do the talking. We'll have a smoke afterwards.'

Charles Tyler introduced himself saying, 'Good morning, ladies.'

They were in the front room of Cynthia's large house, one of the four rooms that she and her friend Stella used in this 25 room mansion. The apartment out the back was occupied by Cynthia's son Francis when he was in Melbourne. Stella poured Tyler some tea and added milk and sugar at his request, balancing a biscuit on the saucer.

'Beautiful location,' he said, munching the biscuit, flicking crumbs off his bright red tie. 'You can see the river but you can't hear the freeway. Beautiful. It's all about position, you know.' And he munched. 'Hot out there this morning. You've got a nice bit of shade in the garden though. Wonderful old trees.'

Cynthia sipped and lowered her cup. 'The point is, Mr Tyler, as I told you on the telephone, we don't intend to sell. So you could have saved yourself the trouble of coming out here.'

'Call me Charles, Mrs Meadows. May I call you Cynthia? It's not about buying or selling. That's not what we do.' He shook his head. 'No, no, no.' He sighed. 'I'll explain how we work, OK? I've been through this with your son, Francis.'

Tyler unclipped his briefcase and slid a shiny brochure onto the table. Its slick cover showed an Egyptian pyramid against a dramatic sunset on a sea of sand.

'We like that picture because it shows what can be achieved for posterity by astute property improvement. Can you imagine? Just a desert, some camels, a few Arabs and a couple of palm trees. Then this!' He turned a page and there was a graph, the red line angling dramatically upwards. No more pyramids. These were pictures of old houses, some on overgrown blocks, alongside photographs of gleaming condominiums.

'This is the sort of thing we do,' he said. 'Right across the country right now, there's close to eight hundred million dollars' worth of property being transformed by Tyler Property.'

Cynthia placed her empty cup on the saucer and leaned back in her chair, crossing her arms.

'Mr Tyler. We're not selling.'

Tyler ignored her. 'I was reminded the other day of something old Stanley Meadows said once. It was at the opening of the Meadows Community Centre in Alfred Street back in the '80s. Must have been close to death. Old Mr Meadows said, "The responsibility of any generation is to secure a solid foundation for the next." Those words have stuck with me, Cynthia. They have guided me. He was a great man, Stanley Meadows. And his son, your late husband followed in his footsteps, of course.'

Cynthia rolled her eyes.

'Stanley is remembered as a great councillor, a respected and much-loved community leader, and above all, a gentleman.'

'He was a bastard,' said Cynthia softly. 'They were both bastards. It runs in the Meadows family.'

'It's in the spirit of Stanley Meadows that we've taken the liberty of putting together this proposal.'

With that, and a gentle flourish, Tyler opened the brochure to the middle pages. Across these pages was an 'artist's impression' of a vast residential development, clusters of units, town houses, community areas, the grounds peopled with roughly drawn figures strolling among scratchy grey-green pen marks representing beds of vegetation. Ranged across the top of the fold-out spread were the words: 'The Meadows World. Quality & Community.'

'Quality and community,' Tyler said in a solemn voice almost like praying, his hands clasped, his eyes focused into the distance. 'Quality and community. The values Stanley Meadows lived and breathed.'

Cynthia snorted. 'Values? Stanley Meadows? You've got the wrong bloke there, mister. Look, Mr Tyler …'

'Call me Charles, please. And we like the word 'Meadows' from the marketing perspective. Your family name of course, a link with history, but also the image of peace, nature, serenity.'

'Mr Tyler, we are not selling.'

'Yes, I understand Cynthia, and we are not buying. We form business partnerships with people. Beneficial partnerships that provide full equity to all, yourself and your son. We are not buyers. We are business partners.'

And so the discussion progressed. Tyler talking, Cynthia yawning, Stella nodding into her little nap, the Jack Russell settling on her lap. Finally, Tyler clipped his briefcase and stood to go, leaving the brochure on the table.

'I'll leave that for you to read at your leisure. I've been through it with Francis and he's happy, but says his mum's got a mind of her own. And I'm glad to hear that.' He provided an oily smile and swung his briefcase from the table.

Cynthia carried the tea set on a tray to the kitchen and returned with a pack of tobacco, an old cigar box containing marijuana, papers and a lighter. Stella was suddenly awake. She shuffled to a louvred window to open a pane, and set an ashtray on a small table before the window seat, as she always did. Cynthia passed the joint to Stella, following a ritual of more than forty years. Stella took a long draw of the smoke, returned it to Cynthia and broke out her knitting from a battered cane basket with handles sheathed in crochet work.

Through gaps in the trees, Cynthia could make out the towers of apartment blocks in a patch of sky where once only church spires had dared intrude. She stood slowly and walked to the fire-place over which hung a massive gilt-framed mirror surrounded by monochrome photographs of young men, arms crossed, in football outfits. Old fashioned hand lettering across the base explained the mirror had been presented to 'The Hon. Councillor Stanley Meadows', for his encouragement and support. In other words, a few hundred pounds.

All of them dead now. Even their kids were dead. That was Cynthia's generation. Some still alive, in care, poor souls, dribbling and demented. Not even eighty some of them.

The two women left the house for the garden where they lounged on cane chairs, Stella at her knitting, Cynthia tapping at her laptop.

'You've been very remote, love, the last week,' Stella said. 'What's on your mind?'

'This is important, Stella, a big project. We'll have to get everyone onside. I know how to do it but it's got to be professional. Like I used to do things in business. No half measures.'

A team of men were in the house following instructions to polish floors, scrub walls, remove the furniture from the old ballroom and leave it clear for Adrian Alford of 'Double A Interiors'. Cynthia and Adrian had agreed on white leather, glass and blond wood. The designer had imagined two distinct spaces in the ballroom. His sketches showed one corner of the room, chairs close, intimate lighting from a pair of lamps, a low bar and a Kashmiri rug; then a space at the far end of the room with a long glass-topped table and elegant seating for twelve and a large wall-mounted screen.

There was psychology to the design. A person seated with a group at the long table could glimpse a more intimate space that gave the promise, perhaps, of more intimate meetings if discussions were to advance. While individuals ushered directly to the intimate space would feel at once the privilege of their position and the power of an organisation accustomed to large conferences. It was 'business bullshit, design rule number one,' as Cynthia explained to Stella.

'We'll be having some minor meetings,' Cynthia said. 'Just to get everyone warmed up. Then the one big bash where they all come together. It'll be like the '80s all over again, when we were doing those Gold Coast developments. Bring the sharks together with the money, let them mix and whet their appetites, and you get a nice kind of frenzy.'

Stella nodded. 'Of course. Some meetings. But for the life of me Cynthia, I don't understand what for?'

'I've decided to do the development myself. As well as the apartments and townhouses, we'll have a small retirement home for you and me and a few friends out the back looking over the river. Pool and sauna, gymnasium with a personal trainer, that kind of thing.'

'I don't understand,' Stella said, her eyes on the line of wool twisting through her fingers. 'Francis was saying that he had everything planned for us, once the house was sold. We'd both move to that retirement place in Brighton.'

'Don't worry about Francis,' said Cynthia. 'Your children always think they know what's best for you. Francis is another lying Meadows male. Think yourself lucky you didn't have any children, Stella.'

She closed the lid of the laptop and stood, stretching her arms upward in a yoga pose.

'Stella, it's very simple. I don't want to move. You don't want to move. But you and I can't stay in this big dump as it is. An aged-care place makes sense. But we don't want someone else's idea of aged-care, do we? We could build our own right here, financed by the real estate. We could have our own music, people we like, yoga, drama performances, a nice bar, some restaurants. Right here. You could get your old jazz quartet together.'

Stella winced. 'They're all dead, except Kenny.'

'Well, a duo then.'

'Kenny's got dementia.'

'Oh, for Christ's sake, Stella, put him on fucking drums. We're not dead yet. I'm going down in style, just watch it.'

'Cynthia, Francis seemed to have it worked out that we are going into that nice home he showed us. You are being naughty.'

Cynthia ignored her.

'Remember when Kevin and I were in business back then and it started to fly? It was me who did all the thinking. I know how to do it. It's called venture capital. The Tyler people have done the hard work, got the plans, manipulated the council. We'll buy them out, that's what we'll do.'

Cynthia flipped open the laptop and scrolled down a few pages, standing behind the screen, moving her balance from one leg to another.

'Here it is,' she said, finding the item regarding Tyler Property. 'A division of Tyler Capital ... owned by ... let me see ... owned by ... Lanski Asset Management. Vance Lanski, ex-partner of Carla Manetti? Yes.'

Stella shrugged her shoulders which was perhaps one gesture softer than rolling her eyes.

'Your one big asset is this property,' Stella said. 'But it's not enough to develop a bloody suburb. And Francis has got it all worked out for us, he told you, Cynthia. He is looking after you. Us.'

'No, Stella, you are getting things wrong again. It's me who's sorting this out, not Francis. Francis has moved to New York. He's another bastard Meadows male. Stella, what you don't realise, what Francis can't see and these real estate creeps couldn't begin to imagine, is I've got another asset that's potentially a lot bigger than this house, this block, this suburb. It's contacts. I know people who can do it. I have contacts. All over the world. That is worth real money, Stella. Folding money. You watch me, sweetheart.'

A few weeks later, towards evening, at that time when the low sun showed off the reds and browns of autumn and the air was spiced with grassy fragrances, Stella fussed with an ice bucket and glasses, several bowls of nuts and an arrangement of fruit from Halliday's in Armadale. Carl, the hired butler, looked over the flower arrangements.

Cynthia greeted her few guests with a breathy hello and a two-cheek-kiss in the arched entrance to the conservatory. She wore tapered, tight black slacks and a greenish grey-gold silk top that flowed across her shoulders. The woman at Kinesa's Boutique had told her it was called Tutankhamen Gold.

Earlier in the day, Cynthia's hairdresser, Maurice, had cropped her hair tight at the sides and left a random spiked ridge along the crown at the top and tousled at the front. The colourist had called the shade a deep scarlet and had tipped the spikes in a subtly darker shade. Blood tips, she called them.

'When Carla arrives she won't eat anything,' Cynthia said, floating a silk-draped arm across the table, lots of silver on her wrist, Egyptian style. Plenty of Nefertiti to go with the Tutankhamen. 'Doesn't matter. We'll just drink champagne. I think it's perfect that you join us, Stel,' Cynthia said. 'To get a real feel for this project. Business can be very exciting.'

Then the familiar tearful cry of the old iron gate as it swung open, and the gentle gravel crackle.

'It's an Aston Martin,' said Cynthia catching a glint of metal as it passed the conservatory. 'She always has one when she's in town.' Stella poured herself another bubbly.

'Dear Carla, darling.' Kisses on cheeks. Carla was a younger woman with a dramatic appearance, lean, tanned, dark around the eyes.

'It's been so long. Marvellous, marvellous. A drink in the conservatory, then to business.' Inside the house where the offices would be, tools and tarps were scattered, buckets and polishing machines.

'So, Carla, this will be the head office, conference area over there, long table, video etcetera.'

The three women found comfortable seats around a low glass table where the butler had placed the ice bucket, and then retired to hover.

'I'm looking at getting into bed with some capital,' said Cynthia, 'so I thought we'd catch up and I'd pick your brains. Carla, I'm not after an investment from Manetti, of course. But I know you'd just know who to talk to. Just looking at options, really. Broad spectrum stuff. We've got one company we're looking at. Real estate, mining interests, retail chain. Under the one roof and a possible float.'

Carla had built up the Meadow's investment business and then branched out on her own and took off. Kevin would shake his head and call her a cowgirl. Giving business a bad name, he had said. She appealed to Cynthia. Kevin was a bore.

'Your timing could be good,' Carla said. 'There's a lot of money around looking for a place to go. Asian money, interested in safety, you know. Of course you've got the grey areas … high returns, and … the waters get a bit muddy sometimes. But it's money, looking for a home.'

Money looking for a home, thought Stella smiling to herself. Just like me. Nice, safe home, quiet environment, that's what the money seemed to be looking for. A common need, apparently. She was guzzling the champagne, the butler was refilling her glass, the effects of the earlier joint were still lingering. And she was listening to a strange language.

Stella stirred, the dog wriggled in her lap. 'Sorry Cynthia, I must have nodded off.'

'Stella, this is delicious. Maybe Tony Lo will do the money. Chinese money. Carla will manage the whole deal. It will be a float, we will buy out Tyler, and you and I will have our own retirement home on the Yarra. It's a glorious result, Stel.'

Stella smiled and nodded. 'Yes,' she said, 'it is.'

The next day, Cynthia awoke fresh from exuberant dreams. She showered, dressed and followed the sound of tea cups to the kitchen. In the hallway were suitcases. More suitcases. Francis coming home? But no. They were her suitcases.

And Stella's old suitcases.

From the ballroom, she heard the voice of her son echoing around the family history's walls,

'Mum, is that you?' She heard the child in him; that funny, wise, loving, always-wondering voice, and she almost stooped down to sweep the boy into her arms. The same smile appeared, now attached to a tall man, walking along the hall towards her, his arms wide to embrace. His blue eyes smiling right at her like a power that could fix anything. Familial kisses.

'We'll have some tea later, Stella,' Francis called down the hall.

His eyes tightened on his mother's face. Up close, he could see the blotched mascara, the skewed lip liner, the thick and patchy rouge and pancake that caked the cracks and crowned a lizard neck. The smile sunk from her lips, her cheeks seemed to have lost their body, falling into skeletal hollows. Beneath the paint he saw the faint pencil sketch of an old woman, barely there. Francis grasped his mother's wrist, thin to the bone, and led her cruelly, almost dragged her, into the ballroom.

Low morning light shafted through those tall windows and there were tarpaulins, plastic buckets, scattered power tools, cables, sanding machines. Francis Meadows was standing there, breathing furiously, frowning down at his mother. Where Stanley Meadows once shook his hips and danced the foxtrot, his grandson Francis simply shook his head.

'Mum, what the hell is going on here?' He spoke softly, his palms facing upwards in a shrug, looking around the room that was an abandoned workplace.

'Darling, it will be so cool,' Cynthia giggled, fluttering her badly attached lashes. She gestured with a thin arm that shook as she tried awkwardly to flip her wrist with elegance.

'Over there on the far wall,' she said, 'will be a kind of media centre. Lots of screens and, well, you know, a buzz. People doing stuff. Things happening. Conferences, presentations to investors. Where we are standing here will be the hub ... the conversation area for deep talk. Getting the deal done. Baby, I am so pleased this is coming together.'

Francis's jaws were clenching and he wagged his head with a forced, puzzled smile.

'What, Mum?'

'Oh, I'm sorry Francis, I haven't brought you up to date. It's moving so fast. Those people who wanted to buy the house ... Tyler?'

'Tyler Properties, yes. I asked them to talk to you, Mum. They're going to develop the house and property, pay off our debts, clear some capital for your future, and let us retain some equity in the property as an investment.'

'No, no. We've moved on Francis. We're now creating an investment consortium to buy out the holding company. The company that owns Tyler. So we own it, develop this property ourselves, town houses. Plus a retirement village for me and Stella and some people we like.'

'Mum. Mum!' Francis closed his eyes, raised his hands to his head and slowly turned a full circle in the middle of the ballroom.

'We've spoken about this, Mum. You're moving to Park Cheney in Brighton. You know this.'

'I know you. You bugger off to New York and leave Stella and me to look after ourselves, so that's what we're doing. Using our wits.'

'Mum, we fixed it before I went to New York. We had lunch, remember, we went down to see Park Cheney and signed the papers, and then we had lunch at Mario's. Remember? You were worried about Stella and I went to see her sister.'

'Stella's not going to live with her sister.' Cynthia raised her voice. 'The sister hasn't got the space. Hasn't got the money. Stella's staying right here with me.'

'Yes, Mum, I spoke to her sister. Stella is staying with you and she is moving with you to Park Cheney. Remember? We've arranged to loan them the bond so she can afford it. Jesus, Mum. Don't you remember?'

'You're just like your father. What about all the plans I've made? Just because you didn't think of it. A typical Meadows male you are. Anyway, it's all fixed. I spoke to Carla Manetti last night. We've got Linus Ho Ling stitched. Chinese money. The whole thing works, we can do a float, buy out Tyler ...'

'Jesus fucking Christ!'

'Tea is ready.' Stella had put on a sweet, disarming, sing-song voice. She hung in the doorway with a smile, challenging them to continue the argument. Mother and son were silent, glaring at each other, then turned and followed Stella to the kitchen.

'We were just going through the timeline,' Francis said to Stella as they settled at the table.

There was a large oval plate of scones that Stella had baked that morning. Baking smells were in the air along with the gentle fragrance of the tea. Francis lifted his cup and slowly returned it to the saucer without sipping.

'What it looks like,' he said to Stella, 'is an interim move to Park Cheney down in Brighton for you and Mum while the ends are all tied up on Mum's business plan. Capital-raising will take maybe six months. I'll get my lawyers to put together a notice of intent. Talk to Carla further about the investment package. There's no need for offices here. We'll do all that through Manetti. The lengthy part, of course, will be planning permits. Could be a year. There's bound to be objections; it all takes time. Planning tribunal, assessment, more time. Construction, another two or three years. Fit out, finishing. Always takes time. Always runs overtime. A good six or seven years, it looks like. Meanwhile you two have to be happy.'

Stella nodded and smiled. 'Time,' she said, 'it's always time that gets you, isn't it?'

She sipped her tea and looked across at Cynthia. Her friend's head was down, chin toward breast. The bottom rim of her eyes had reddened with the glisten of tears and her mascara had run. The uncombed slept-in hairstyle was spiked up in untidy red tufts along one side.

Francis backed the Range Rover up to the front veranda and his assistants loaded the suitcases. The understanding was that Cynthia would go ahead and Stella would follow once she'd sorted out her wardrobe and jewellery.

Stella helped Cynthia gather some of her last things from her room and they stood by the front door. As Cynthia buried her face in Stella's shoulder, the other woman softly kissed her hair.

The car pulled out of the driveway and stopped. Francis looked around to the rear seat as Cynthia opened the car door.

'I'll close the gate,' she said.

THE REVEREND TIMOTHY'S TEMPTATION

Lawrence Goodstone

Timothy had been vicar at Saint Thomas's church for almost five years. The parish he served was situated in a decaying residential area of inner Sydney. The suburbs making up the parish had once been relatively prosperous but as its upwardly mobile denizens moved to larger properties in western and southern Sydney, local infrastructure was left to decay and the area's reputation sank slowly into the cracked paving and potholed roads which held the streets together in a web of clogged arteries.

Timothy was given a choice. He was a bright, young energetic priest who graduated from his studies with a boundless enthusiasm. The church hierarchy initially offered him a parish on Sydney's upper north shore which housed an ageing but wealthy and supportive congregation, but Timothy took up the alternative offer of Saint Thomas's, which was desperately trying to hang onto its dwindling flock of worshippers after the former vicar retired. Timothy grabbed the challenge with both hands. He was sure he could energise enough locals to renew their relationship with the church and saw hope in some of the youth who were desperately looking for a mentor to inject hope into their aimless lives.

Added to this, was his new wife, Emily, who shared her new husband's zeal and who was prepared to roll up her sleeves and help him in any way possible. At first the tiny, historic, run down vicarage presented as a challenge. It would be fun to renovate it on a shoestring and turn it into a warm, welcoming home but as the years slid by, the lights dimmed for both the Reverend Timothy and his lovely Emily. Recruiting new congregants transpired to be akin to pulling teeth and as for the youth of the area, Timothy reluctantly and sadly had all but given up on coaxing them into redemption. To make matters worse, the church's weary Board of Governors, although appreciating Timothy's efforts, had become risk averse and held the view that what little money they had in their coffers was not worth wasting on a doomed enterprise. All of this had taken a toll on both Timothy and Emily. Timothy had become obsessed with the church's slow physical deterioration and spent too much of his valuable spare time patching up leaks and fighting a losing battle with the local rodent population. For her part, Emily tried hard to lift Timothy's sagging spirits but just getting by on his modest stipend and the challenges of raising a toddler and a baby in quite primitive conditions began to show signs of impacting on their hitherto rock-solid relationship.

On a drab, wintry evening with the children finally asleep, Emily served dinner. The wind outside seemed ingenious in finding nooks and crannies in the old building's roof and gables which enabled it to produce an orchestra of intrusive sounds. Emily did everything she could think of to cheer up the room. On this occasion, she'd lit candles in two antique candlesticks which she'd found in the vestry and placed them on the rough-hewn table on which they ate their meals. She thought it might bring a little romance to proceedings but draughts from every direction thwarted her intent and the candles kept blowing out.

'Never mind Emily, it was a lovely idea. I appreciate the thought.' Timothy rose from his chair, pulled his wife against him and buried his face in her neck. 'I knew it would be hard but I didn't think it would be this hard.'

'I know, Timmy. It's not your fault and I don't blame you. You've given it your best shot but perhaps it's time to seek out new pastures. I'm sure the church would see it as perfectly reasonable for you to want to move on. Our sons are little and as long as they are loved and cared for, that's all they want for now. But soon, they'll want to run around and explore, and this area ...' She stopped herself. She'd taken it far enough.

Timothy returned to his seat at the table. He clasped his hands in front of him and sat hunched over. 'I know, Emmy. You're right. But the church had such high expectations of me and if we leave, it will be the death knell for the parish.'

Emily brought two plates to the table. 'Let's just think about it, my darling. We don't have to rush into anything but I refuse to see you and us sink into a quicksand out of which there's no return. Anyway, eat up. I hope this hot pot's edible because I could only afford a cheap cut of meat.'

Timothy looked at his wife. She was still beautiful but fatigue had begun to edge into her delicate features. His eyes misted over.

Emily reached across the table and covered his hand with hers. 'You don't have to apologise. I love you and will always be at your side.'

The meal was eaten in a loving but troubled silence.

That night Timothy woke with a start. He glanced at the bedside clock which showed '2.32' on its luminous dial. Emily lay alongside him breathing deeply and evenly. Her long hair was spread across her pillow. They had made urgent but restrained love for fear of waking the children. This woman was Timothy's everything. If there was one thing which he constantly thanked god for it was having Emily in his life. And she had given him two perfect and adorable boys. His little family deserved better than was on offer but he was confused and indecisive about what to do in the situation. As these thoughts skittered across his consciousness, he raised himself on one elbow. Something had woken him. Was it traffic noise? Was it local youths messing around in the church grounds? Was it the blessed wind playing tricks again? He listened. He thought he heard muffled voices. It sounded like people arguing underwater. Then there were a series of barely distinguishable thuds followed by a car driving off. He lay still. Should he go and investigate? To do so would almost certainly wake Emily and her precious sleep would be fractured. As he vacillated, all went quiet. He waited a few more minutes then decided any investigation could wait until morning.

Timothy woke early. Mercifully the children had not yet begun their dawn chorus. It was a little after six thirty and the grey beams of winter light crept through the imperfections in the curtains. He eased himself out of bed, grabbed his clothes and tiptoed into the cold kitchen, where he dressed. Pulling on a quilted jacket, he carefully unlocked the rear door of the vicarage and, using the old, original hand-forged key, closed the door knowing that any click might wake Emily or, more likely, wake his children who had more acute hearing than most wild animals in the jungle. He walked around the building not quite knowing what he expected to find and as he returned to where he'd started, he wasn't surprised that there was nothing untoward to be seen. He moved to open the door to return inside but on the spur of the moment he decided to walk around the small, slightly unkempt graveyard which hosted a few dozen historical graves. Most of his parishioners who had died on his watch had opted for cremation, the rest preferring to be buried in various cemeteries outside of the parish. It was as if the tired old area was not even acceptable to the dead. The headstones in the graveyard, telling of many infant deaths and adults taken long before their prime, were only of interest to some amateur historians. A biting early morning wind caused Timothy to pull his jacket tight around his body. As he came to the end row of graves, he saw something behind one of them which at first looked like a small bundle of wood. On closer inspection it turned out to be a dilapidated, rectangular wooden box about the size of a shoe box. At first, he assumed it was rubbish left by a lazy local who couldn't be bothered to find a garbage bin.

He kicked it gently with his foot but it hardly moved. Timothy mused that it was either embedded in the soil because it had been there for a long time or that it had something in it. He crouched down and lifted the box, which had a crude latch but no padlock. His worst fear was that it would contain a stillborn foetus or a clutch of suffocated new-born kittens. Curiosity being what it is, he could only allay his anxiety by opening it. He quietly thought up a prayer, hoping that the box would not contain evidence of someone's tragedy or evil deed. He began to feel a little silly, harbouring such melodramatic thoughts. The box was probably filled with gardening tools left by old Billy, an octogenarian parishioner who voluntarily tended the church grounds when he had the energy. Timothy flicked open the latch and lifted the lid.

What he saw did not register at first. He blinked and looked again. The box had a wooden middle divider. One side of the box contained wad after wad of what appeared to be fifty-dollar notes, each bundle encased in a thick rubber band. There were two layers of notes, and Timothy knew immediately that he was holding thousands of dollars – perhaps tens of thousands of dollars. On the other side of the divider was a large plastic bag taking up the whole of the compartment. Although the plastic was opaque, Timothy could see the bag contained a white powder which at first looked like flour. Although a man of the cloth, Timothy was not totally naïve and was sufficiently worldly to realise immediately that the powder was likely to be an illegal drug, probably cocaine. His mind was racing. What he'd come across was a serious drug stash, possibly dropped in haste. Then he remembered the strange noises which had woken him.

As he stood shivering in the bleak graveyard, he couldn't help but think that he must have entered an episode of a television crime drama. Someone was sure to return to collect the box and that could be at any moment. He had no wish to be part of such a confrontation. His second thought was that he should immediately call the police. His mobile telephone was in the vicarage. Should he replace the box where he'd found it? Is that what the police would want? Or should he take it with him into the house while he made the call? He decided on the second option and after glancing around to see whether anyone had been watching, he closed the box and made towards the rear door of the building which would take him into the kitchen.

Once inside, he placed the box on the table which still displayed evidence of the previous night's dinner. Having forgotten to charge the battery the night before, his mobile phone was dead. He looked at the yellowing landline telephone which hung on the wall. He hardly used the landline these days and frequently asked himself why he continued to pay the rent required. He seemed mesmerised, alternating his gaze between the box and the telephone.

With some hesitancy, he reached up to a shelf for the book in which Emily had carefully recorded telephone numbers they may require. He flicked to the page which documented a series of local and centralised police related numbers. It was now nearly seven o'clock and he could hear sounds of the children stirring. Perhaps he should wait until Emily emerged to bring her into the picture.

He heard his wife in loving early morning conversation with the little ones and their excited responses. He'd tell Emily what had occurred then call the local police station. The problem was that as a result of his community activities, he knew the hierarchy at the local command. He also knew through other sources that an investigation was underway into certain alleged dubious activities at the station which had been brought to the attention of the Police Department's Integrity Unit and that senior personnel, who he knew quite well, were under a cloud. He was obliged to work with local police but he wasn't obliged to like them. He had found the most senior police officers to be cavalier in dealing with local crime-related issues and dismissive of suggestions by some community leaders that a hint of discrimination and prejudice frequently pervaded police procedures. When he had tried to raise these matters diplomatically at appropriate local forums, he was gently and patronisingly slapped down in that blokey supercilious manner perfected by overweight, middle-aged police officers whose training had come to them on the streets rather than from the professional courses on offer at the Goulburn Police Academy. As these thoughts raced through Timothy's mind he could hear the clatter of feet on the stairs and clamouring voices demanding breakfast.

'Daddy, where are you?' Harry, his three-year-old, shouted.

Timothy heard Emily's slippers clip-clopping on the wooden stairs, the sound accompanied by Jamie, the twenty-month-old, repeating over and over, 'Dada, Dada, where you?'

Then without thinking, and acting purely on instinct, the Reverend Timothy grabbed the box off the table and hurried into the adjoining vestry where he placed it on the floor behind a dusty, now obsolete, altar. He re-entered the kitchen trying, somewhat unsuccessfully, to look nonchalant.

Emily was quizzical. She took a long look at her husband. 'What on earth have you been doing down here? We've heard doors opening and some odd noises. Have you been moving furniture at this ungodly hour? Sorry, if that sounds blasphemous.'

'Sorry, Emmy. I tried to make no noise. I … I … I was just looking for the old lectern in the vestry. I thought I might polish it up and give it a run.'

Timothy had no idea where this fib emanated from and felt immediately guilty that his wife should be its recipient.

'Why would you be doing that at such an unearthly hour?'

Timothy shrugged. 'I woke early and just couldn't get back to sleep so I …'

Emily gently interrupted him. 'Anyway, doesn't matter. Now that you're here, you can help get the children's breakfasts.'

Timothy welcomed the distraction and for the next forty-five minutes or so, normal family activities took over. At the conclusion of proceedings, Timothy kissed Emily lightly on the cheek. 'Emmy, if it's OK with you, I'm off to my office to spend a little time preparing Sunday's sermon.'

Emmy nodded acquiescence, and Timothy kissed his children before making for his cramped office. On the way, he glanced out of the dusty hallway window which overlooked the graveyard. It was empty as usual. The only movement was the rustling of the sparse, brittle leaves on two old, gnarled gum trees. He furtively opened the door to the vestry and checked that the box lay where he'd placed it. He then went into his office, such as it was, sat down at the desk which had been there since the church had been consecrated, placed his chin in his cupped hands and pondered. In the quiet of the room all manner of thoughts bounced around in his head.

One minute he thought like a servant of god examining his options in terms of morality and what was the right thing to do. Then his thoughts took on a more primitive aspect. What would be best for his family for whom he was responsible? What would the community want him to do? Would the church hierarchy expect him to do the obvious? Would they say one thing but mean another? In his confused state, a reluctant memory slowly and disturbingly materialised, a memory which he'd tried hard to repress. The fact that it came to him now should have been a warning but it only added to his confusion.

An image came to him of his sixteen-year-old self. Together with another boy, who his parents had warned him about, he had climbed into the rear window of the local newsagent's shop. It was done on a dare and Timothy led the way. He remembered stuffing his pockets with various items, none of which he wanted or were of any real use to him. His fellow thief, who was obviously more experienced, proceeded to wipe away fingerprints. After they'd made their getaway, Timothy was wracked by guilt. On the one hand, he'd proven a misguided sense of bravery to his accomplice who held sway in the schoolyard. On the other hand, his actions went against his natural inclination to abhor such behaviour. The incident was never mentioned again but the memory never left Timothy and as the years passed and he gravitated towards a career in the church, he occasionally doubted his suitability for the calling, accusing himself of being morally flawed.

His head felt like it would explode. Then it came to him! What would Jesus expect of him? Would his saviour see any decision as personal or would he expect his representative to look to the greater good? Timothy shook himself. He stood up and paced the tiny room. Why was he even contemplating options? It was obvious. He had an obligation to hand the box to the authorities. But he knew how things worked. At least he thought he knew from gossip and innuendo. If he handed the box to the police, even if he took it to headquarters, the money would ultimately go into government coffers where it would disperse like a bucket of water poured into an ocean. As for the drugs, they might be incinerated. But would they? Could he be sure quantities wouldn't be skimmed off for nefarious purposes? Hadn't he heard that drugs were traded by opportunistic police for information or that some police were actually dealers? Should he take out the money and replace the box where he'd found it? Whoever left it there could hardly assume it was Timothy who had found it. If they got their drugs back that might be the end of it.

Then Timothy began fantasising on what he could do with the money. Like the good person he basically was, his first thought was for the church. In order not to raise suspicions, improvements could be undertaken incrementally. Up to a point, monies could be attributed to anonymous donors. The Board of Governors would be mesmerised by their good fortune so that any examination of the money's source would be undertaken with a light touch. The Board would be more interested in protecting the anonymous source. Timothy smiled to himself. Was not the Mafia one of the greatest benefactors to the Catholic Church?

Timothy sat down at the desk again. He stared at the large King Charles bible which took pride and place on the faded leather desktop. His parents had given him the bible with pride as a present when he graduated from theological college. What would they say if they knew what he was contemplating?

Then there was his new family. Would it be totally immoral, let alone corrupt, for his family to profit from the windfall? He was not thinking of personal gain but simply improving conditions at the vicarage. It could be reasoned that this would be a benefit to the church and that his wife and children would only enjoy any advantage by default. He thought how happier and more contented Emily would be if she could just enjoy a few improvements to make her life easier. She was not one who hankered for luxuries but what she wouldn't give for a washing machine that didn't break down every few months, for a dryer rather than a clothesline to provide a more accessible supply of children's clothes, and a dishwasher which would save her time and spare her hands. As Timothy thought, he vacillated. One moment he considered his thoughts deranged, the next moment he saw a pragmatism in a 'Robin Hood' approach. What if the truth came out? Would he or could he be charged with stealing? How could it be stealing if the money had no owners? Wasn't there a charge based on having goods or money thought to have been stolen or illegally obtained? Or should he just hand the money and drugs in and be done with it? This was the easiest and least problematic of the options but would do nothing for his life or his church.

Then he decided. He would not make an immediate decision. He would leave things as they were for a day, maybe two. He could control his own fate. Nobody else knew anything of this and that's the way he'd keep it. At least until he'd made his choice. He opened the bible. Maybe he would find the answer there. He tried to conjure up a theme for Sunday's sermon but it troubled him that as a man of the cloth, he began to feel a bit of a fraud. Perhaps Emily was right. Perhaps what he needed was a change of parish. This would reinvigorate him. The box and its contents would leave a stain on him for life.

As this and other thoughts confused and disturbed him, there was a gentle knock on the door. Timothy was almost relieved by the interruption. He stood and opened the door. Emily was holding baby Jamie but there was something about her look that did not feel quite right. Timothy stroked Jamie's head.

'Is everything all right?'

Emily stared at Timothy. 'I don't know.'

'What do you mean you don't know? Where's Harry? Is he OK on his own?'

'Timothy, there are two men in the kitchen. They knocked at the back door and ...' She paused. She seemed lost for words.

'Emmy, what do you mean two men? Who are they? What do they want? Have you left Harry with them?'

'They're not parishioners. I don't know who they are. They sort of invited themselves in. They said they want to speak to you. One of them put Harry on his knee and pretended to play with him but ... Timmy, I don't like the look of them. I don't like the way the big one put Harry on his knee.' Emily clutched Jamie tight. 'Timmy, I'm a little scared.'

'Emmy, my darling, stay here with the baby and don't leave this room. Now listen to me. Emmy, stay calm. I'm sure there's absolutely nothing wrong but just in case, I want you to lock the door after I go out and if you hear anything – anything at all which worries you – call the police from your mobile. It's on the desk here. Don't ask me any questions. Please, my darling, just do as I say. They're probably some locals who want something or other, but just in case.'

Emily gazed at her husband wide-eyed but before she could respond, Timothy was out through the door, which he closed after him. He waited a moment until he heard the click of the lock.

Before making for the kitchen, Timothy made a detour into the vestry. He pulled the box from behind the old altar. Then he glanced up at the wall where a small wooden Christ looked down on him. Tears welled in Timothy's eyes. He dropped to one knee. 'Please forgive me Lord! I've doubted myself but I don't doubt you.'

He stood up and, holding the box, walked urgently towards the kitchen.

WORDS FOR SAM

Carolyn Thrum

'What is she saying?'

'I don't know. I wish I did. She hasn't said a word I can understand since she arrived a week ago.'

Kate, aged five, looked up at the newcomer with the words, 'Oobiada sookilala'.

The visitor, a stout woman with a veined face and a club-like nose, bent down with her hands on her hips over the girl. 'What does that mean? Can't you speak English?'

Kate stood as still as she could with her arms by her sides and stared at the visitor's shoes, thinking, toe peeper creepers, her fat toenails painted cherry berry red the same colour as her lips.

'Leave her Maisie! She's missing her brother. He's only been gone two months.'

At the mention of her brother Sam, Kate ran from the room. She sat on the edge of the strange bed, now hers, and smelt the musty locked away from the world smell of the faded pink and threadbare chenille bed cover. She ran her fingers over its rippled surface.

The girl was small for her age, 'toothpick legs and arms', Sam called them. Her hair was the colour of wet golden beach sand and she had a fine sprinkling of freckles over her nose. Her grandfather – 'Pa' to her – called them fairy kisses and she wondered when the fairies had given them to her. She hadn't felt a thing.

'Bayada, bayadum,' she whispered to her brother's memory. He would understand that she was saying goodbye even if no one else did.

'Sam, you shouldn't have left me like you did.' Kate spoke to the silent room. 'You were s'posed to wait for me. Pa always said you should wait so why did you run ahead? I couldn't keep up with you when you disappeared. I called, "Puttaya ballaya Massie". But you didn't wait. I called and called you Massie until my voice ran out. I was so scared but Pa told me always to wait if I got lost so I went to sleep under a tree.'

Some strangers who were out searching for her woke her the next morning and took her to Pa. 'Sam is hiding from me,' she said to Pa. He was crying and shaking and held her tighter than ever before. Kate was frightened.

'No Katie, Sam is dead,' he said, just like that. 'SAM IS DEAD. He's gone. He fell down a very high cliff and is dead.'

It took three weeks after the funeral for the decision to be made. Grandfather Pa could not bring up a young girl on his own. Kate knew that Pa would send her away.

'I'm sorry,' he said, 'I'll visit you every week. You can come and stay for weekends and holidays.' Kate's heart shifted in her chest. She knew this would not happen. Pa loved Sam best and just put up with her, a girl. Sam had been his fishing mate. Sam had been good at imitating the politicians on television. Pa would laugh and laugh, complaining that his sides were splitting. He'd taught Sam how to whittle sticks and had taken him on walks to look for blackberries to make a pie. Kate didn't complain. She knew they'd been lucky to have Pa.

Most of her life it had only been Pa and Sam. Sam was lucky. He remembered their mother and Pa said it was true that their mother had brought them home to live with him after their father died. She took them shopping and played with them, read them stories and sang to them. But one day she left and Pa said there would just be the three of them in future. And now there were two.

When they asked, 'Pa, what happened to our mother?' his answer was, 'I can't answer that.'

Pa was a trembling mess at the funeral. He sobbed and shook and afterwards drank a lot of whiskey. Kate knew that Pa felt that Sam's death was his fault; that he should have stopped them going onto the cliffs behind the house; not let them run wild. Perhaps he didn't understand. He was after all a grandpa and not a dad. Maybe it would have been better if it had been her and not Sam.

The funeral was held in a little stone chapel on a neighbour's estate. Pa thought that by holding it on private property, he could keep it small but he didn't realise how many people would feel sad at the death of a child. The chapel was full and many had to stand outside in the hot sun. Kate sat holding Pa's unsteady hand while she stared at the small coffin, willing Sam to push open the lid, stand up and say hello to her 'oobiada Takkie'. She whispered and he spoke back to her. She would always be able to talk to Sam.

The sun beat down on the chapel as hot as a bush fire. It was so hot that Kate's best dress stuck to her Every time she stood up she had to pull it back off her legs. The pastor's voice became a blur as the heat filled every space around the mourners. Kate felt faint and dizzy. On the walk back to their house, Pa stumbled and fell down onto his knees. People ran to help him up and she could see the pity on their faces when they looked at her, and she knew that her life would soon change again.

On the Monday a young woman with a long blond plait, pale blue summer dress and long dangly earrings came to their house. She was introduced to Kate as, 'Cleo, the lady who is going to find you someone nice to live with'. (Cleo o meomio) This young woman called Cleo was a social worker. She said she had found a nice woman Mrs Joy Johnson (Joyjo). Kate rolled the words into one in her mouth.

'Is your bag packed? I'll take you there now.' Pa looked as if he might cry as he stood in the door space to the kitchen, watching her.

'It's OK, Pa.' she said, and ran over to hug him. She wrapped her arms around his bony waist. 'I'm ready.' The tears streamed down her face but she made no further sound.

'I'll come and see you soon,' he said holding back his tears. 'You're going to grow into a fine lady but you need a woman to help you do that.'

Kate didn't agree.

Mrs Joy Johnson was not unkind, she just didn't love Kate like her brother and grandfather had. A solid woman with grey-tinged, blond curly hair, Joy was a bit younger than Pa. But she was important as she had the experience of having 'brought up girls to become fine women.' She had short legs and arms and plump fingers with six rings on each hand, cutting into the flesh so the fingers looked like little water balloons. Kate overheard visitor Maisie (lazy daisy) and Joy discussing how much she would receive per week for taking her on. Kate realised that the reason Joy took her into her home was because she would be paid; it was Joy's spending money. Kate wondered why everyone didn't take in a foster child.

Joy told her she was divorced and had two grown up daughters as well as two other grown up foster children (Two lots of spending money). None of them still lived with Joy. Kate liked Brad the best. He was the youngest and was just like she imagined Sam might be if he had reached his twenties. He, like her, loved books and often brought one for her when he called around. But that was before the scandal.

Kate could tell that most of Joy's family didn't like her so when she knew they were coming over she would stay in her room with her books and talk to Sam. She saved Sam's language for night time and times when they were alone.

Joy started Kate at the local school after the Christmas holiday period. It was her first year at school and she was tingling with excitement. Joy bought her a uniform from the school recycle shop and a bag and hat. After two days the teacher, Miss Marion, was surprised she could already read so well.

'Who taught you to read?' she asked

'My brother, Sam.'

'Is he here at this school?'

'No Sam is dead.' Just like that. SAM IS DEAD.

Her teacher was upset by this remark and Kate found she had to comfort her. Taking her hand she said, 'Sorry, Miss Marion. He fell off a cliff three months ago and I'm alone.' And then there was one.

'Someone cares for you? Mrs Johnson?'

'Oh yes, she is a foster carer because Pa can't look after a girl and she brought up girls to become fine women.'

'Oh! Well you are a very clever girl being able to read so well and understand so many words.'

'Sam and I used to make up words from the dictionary. I talk to him and teach him new words now he can't teach me.'

Kate watched as Miss Marion turned with a sad smile and hurried off to the staff room, wiping her cheek with a tissue.

Kate found that as long as she stayed out of Mrs Joy Johnson's way she had the run of the house. There were many unused rooms that had a 'locked up for too long smell'. Many of them had just a bed and a side table in them like a long lost hotel or boarding house, and just like Kate's own room. She imagined them full of people like herself, and Joy collecting her spending money. Kate would run up and down the corridors noiselessly and had turned most of the rooms into secret hideaways like Enid Blyton's Famous Five. In the large back bedroom there were two beds with dark caves underneath, where she hid from the smugglers. She would often swim between the islands, across the polished timber floor or use one of the empty drawers as a boat to navigate across the carpeted waters. She also played in the large wardrobe in one of the side bedrooms, imagining smelling the furs stored in them like Lucy did in Lewis Caroll's, The Lion, The Witch and the Wardrobe, before passing through to Narnia.

But never on Wednesdays as that was Joy's cleaning day; the only day in the week she came into these rooms in the house. Every other day she stayed in the kitchen sewing or chatting to friends like crazy Maisie. She also spent many hours reading women's magazines and cutting out recipes that she never tried. It was as though she planned a more exciting life that had yet to happen. The meals she prepared were simple and plain: a few vegetables and some meat followed by a spoonful of custard and fruit. They would sit either end of the kitchen table and wouldn't speak. Kate would say, 'Thank you, Mrs J.' at the end of the meal and help dry the dishes. Apart from meals, they avoided one another as much as possible, only communicating on practical matters such as school, clothing or Cleo (o-meomio) who called from time to time.

Joy thought Kate was a 'peculiar child'. She told Maisie that Kate had strange thoughts in her head. She had heard her talking to herself at night. Kate's world was lived through the stories and adventures that she read in the books she borrowed, with Miss Marion's help, from the school library. She shared all the stories and new words with Sam, reading aloud to him at night in her room. When Joy told Kate one morning as she brushed and plaited her hair that it was turning red, Kate was delighted. 'Oh maybe I'll look like Anne of Green Gables.'

One weekend Kate went with Joy to see her aged mother in St John's Nursing Home. Joy's mother, Mrs Buckley, was ninety. Kate was very excited as she had never seen anyone so old. Pa was only sixty five. She couldn't believe that skin could gather and fold over so much and she was reminded of the saggy baggy dog next door that was still trying to grow into its skin.

'Mother,' Joy shouted, 'this is Kate, my foster child.'

'Not another one, Joy! Don't you know your limits?' growled Mrs Buckley. Kate smiled at Joy's mother and she smiled back. They understood one another. (Just more spending money).

'Well, she seems nice enough. Come here girl?' Kate went close and looked into her cloudy eyes where the blue was bleeding into the whites. 'How long will you keep her?'

'Until she leaves school, Mum, that's the plan.' Joy was annoyed that she had to reveal this to Kate. You could hear it in her voice.

'We'll see,' Mrs Buckley mumbled as she took Kate's small hand in her bony, arthritic fingers that were clumped like a bunch of question marks. She looked Kate up and down.

Mrs Buckley was seated, or rather lying, on a large green vinyl recliner and Kate wondered if she was able to walk. Her collar bones protruded above the neckline of her dress, presenting a landscape of mountains and valleys where her necklace of large white pearls lay delicately balanced. What was left of her thin hair between patches of a shiny scalp had been died black and one of the nurses had tied a red ribbon around a small clump of it. Kate thought it looked silly. The rest of her long body was hidden under an open weave cotton rug, hospital white with a blue border, top and bottom.

So that's the plan, Kate thought. I'll have to leave like Brad when I finish school. Kate liked Joy's mother. She could tell she was someone she could talk to. Maybe she could visit her by herself.

But like all plans that work while times are good, this one would stumble and fall like Pa did, bringing change, sooner rather than later.

It was hot and humid in the first weeks of the following summer. Kate sat by the front door waiting for Brad to take her for a swimming lesson. Over her blue swimmers, she had on a white T-shirt with the words, 'Kiss me' and a pink heart printed on the front. A bulky towel draped over her shoulders dwarfed her small frame. She spun her swimming goggles around her hand like the propeller of a helicopter. Joy came out from the kitchen, wiping her hands on a tea towel.

'Not today Kate, he's not coming anymore.'

'Why not? He said he'd be here at 10.'

'Just put your towel and swimmers away and find something to play with.'

Kate knew not to keep questioning Joy, but she could see sadness in Joy's eyes. By hovering close to the kitchen, she later overheard Joy on the phone to one of her daughters.

'You can never tell when you take them from broken families. Who would have thought? Brad? What do you mean you suspected, and if you did why didn't you warn me?' Joy had tears in her eyes.

Joy has always liked Brad best. It's because he's a boy, Kate thought. Why do parents and grandparents prefer boys?

Joy caught Kate listening. 'I have to go now.'

'What's wrong with Brad? Is he dead?' Kate asked.

'No, just wait here. The police are coming to talk to you.'

'Are they taking me away? I haven't stolen anything.'

Kate waited in the kitchen and then in her room until 6 pm for the police to arrive. She understood it was a problem with Brad, not her, as she hadn't hurt anyone or stolen anything.

Just before 6 o'clock Pa arrived. She threw her arms around him and held him so tight he had to pull one arm off him and then the other, so he could see her.

'Katie! My, how big you are!' She stared at him, biting her bottom lip and trying not to cry as she studied his weathered face and thin body. His belt was drawn in, bunching up his too large trousers at the waist.

'Katie, I'm going to sit with you while the police ask you some questions. Mrs Johnson will be here too.'

Kate nodded. 'But I didn't do anything wrong.'

'I know. We'll just try to answer the policeman's questions.'

Pa took her hand and sat down; jumping up when he heard the door.

'Is this the young lady?' the policeman asked as he smiled at Kate. She tried to hide behind Pa.

'We can sit in here,' Joy said, leading them into the disused and sparsely furnished living room.

'Now Missie, Kate isn't it? Do you like your friend Brad?'

'Yes'

'Does he take you out by himself?'

'Yes'

'Where do you go?'

'To the movies and the swimming pool.'

'Does Brad teach you swimming?'

'Yes'

'Does he come into the dressing room when you get changed?'

'No, he waits outside. What has he done wrong?'

Pa stood up, frustrated by the questioning and blurted, 'For heaven's sake, just ask her straight out. Has he ever touched you inside your pants?'

'No, never! He's really nice to me. He's my friend.'

'Now that's enough, thank you. I would like some time alone with my granddaughter, if you don't mind.' Joy and the policeman left Pa and Kate sitting on the lounge together.

'You understand what they're asking you, don't you? Has he ever touched you when you have had your clothes off.'

'No, of course not. That's horrible. Can I come home now, Pa?'

'Look, sweetie, you know I can't look after you. I can hardly look after myself. You're doing so well here and look so healthy and grown up.'

'I can look after you.' Pa looked down and smiled. 'You know Pa, I like Brad. Why is everyone asking questions?'

'One of the older girls at the swimming club told the police Brad touched her.'

'He wouldn't do that, I know.'

Pa took her out to Joy who was farewelling the police at the front gate.

'Katie knows exactly what they are asking and Brad is

innocent in her eyes.'

It was another two weeks before Kate heard more about Brad. This time Joy was talking to Maisie in the kitchen. Kate listened from the hallway.

'Two of the thirteen-year-old girls at the swimming club have accused him of sexual assault.'

'I can't imagine Brad would do that, can you?'

'No,' Joy shook her head

'What about Kate?'

'No, he hasn't touched Kate. She was adamant about that. You know her!'

They laughed and Kate wondered what was funny.

That night Kate asked her dead brother Sam in her special language why it was that everyone she loved went away. First her mother left, then Sam, Pa and Brad. Brad had told her that if you wished hard enough, sometimes your wishes came true. She hugged her pillow tight and closed her eyes, then wished and wished for Brad and then her mother to come back. She knew it was no use wishing for Sam or Pa.

'Kate!' Joy called up the hallway, 'phone for you.' Kate threw the pillow aside and then ran down to the kitchen.

'Who is it?'

'It's Brad. I've been talking to him and he wants to say hello.'

'Hello, Brad,' she whispered while Joy stood watching.

'I just wanted to say sorry I haven't been able to take you swimming Katie'

'That's OK. Did you do that sexual assault thing?'

'No Kate. I swear I didn't. The girls were angry because I failed them in their resuscitation test, meaning they'll have to do it again.'

'Will the police put you in gaol?'

'No, the girls have apologised and told the police the truth.'

'So can we go swimming now?'

'No, I don't work for the club anymore. You'll have to get lessons from the new teacher.'

'But I want you to teach me, Brad.'

'Maybe in a few months when this all blows over.'

'I wished and wished, Brad, and it worked.'

'What worked, Kate?'

'You came back.'

'Well, sort of. Thanks for wishing, Kate. Bye for now.'

'Brad's not happy,' Kate told Joy. 'I hope we can make him happy again.' She went to her room and sat on her bed with her legs crossed and her eyes closed.

Sam, you have to help me wish for our mother. I'll try and ask Pa. He must know.

Although she kept pleading, Brad was very careful not to be seen alone with Kate. When he visited the house he explained by saying, 'a little mud always sticks.' Kate thought she understood but still didn't see why she couldn't go with him for a swim.

During the following very cold winter, Pa died of pneumonia. Cleo, the social worker, arrived to tell Kate, now aged seven, that Pa's funeral was to be held in four days' time and she would come and take her. Kate ran straight to her room to tell Sam. Oh,

Massie, PA is DEAD. I wish you were here, she sobbed. Now I've got no one.

Joy knocked softly on the door and gathered Kate into her arms. 'You still have me and we'll go to the funeral together.'

The next day Joy took Kate shopping and bought her shoes and a winter coat to wear to the funeral. Kate tried them on, spinning this way and that in front of the mirror. Kate was sad but excited to be going back to the old house. Pa was laid to rest in the graveyard where Sam was buried, behind the small stone church in the neighbours' estate. Kate kept her head down and tried not to cry as the memories of Sam's funeral crowded her thoughts, like a persistent song that won't go away. A lot of people she remembered came up and said hello.

As they were about to head home, Kate looked up and noticed a woman staring at her. The woman pulled away from the person holding her arm and came over to Kate.

'Soobiyada Takkie,' she whispered. Kate opened her mouth in astonishment. 'Yes, Katie, I'm your mother. They brought me out of hospital to go to Pa's funeral. I've been there since Pa had me placed because he didn't think I was well enough to look after you both. Pa couldn't cope with my illness. I get very sick from time to time.'

'Sam is dead too, but how did you know our words?' Kate asked.

'I taught you and Sam the silly language so we could keep our secrets,' Kate's mother explained.

'I don't think it's silly, and I still talk to Sam.'

'So do I, Katie.'

And then there were two.

CECILIA'S KIND OF LOVE

Clarissa Militante

Cecilia's clothes, personal vanity purse, shoes, books, and bags are sprawled on her bed, and she can't decide which to pack first. On the floor are toys for her stepbrother Mario's kid, a perfume and bag for her Aunt Ellen, a leather belt and branded polo shirt for her Uncle Lermo, some canned goods and chocolates for her other stepbrother Ando, and for her paternal relatives. She will only be staying in the Philippines for two weeks – some days will be spent in the province with her father's relatives – yet she has bought a lot of things for people she might not even have time to see.

Her studio apartment is a mess, but she feels pleasure as she surveys it, always reminding herself that this is her own place, and she's not beholden to anyone here. She has been living in San Francisco for a year, after graduating from college, and being fortunate enough to get a high-paying job as an accountant in a hospital. That was after she left her mother and her family in New Jersey.

She used to have her own room in her adoptive parents'

house in Manila, while her two stepbrothers Mario and Ando shared one of the three bedrooms on the second floor. But she has no distinct memory of that room now. It was like any other teenager's room. It served as her sanctuary - more like her asylum - from her own life back then. She wouldn't come out of her room, especially when she knew that Ando was hovering outside her room, which he often did. He was like a puppy that followed her around. Maybe because she was also his only friend, for he too was an introvert. And she was the only one who could tolerate his fondness for explaining – rambling on about everything he had observed or read, from names of plants and characteristics of insects, to the history of the Catholic Church, or how the speed of a car accelerated and the relativity of time. Yet she did enjoy his monologues sometimes because she learned a lot from him. She had not been very studious in elementary or high school. And there was no-one else she felt comfortable with in his family. She could not accuse her step-parents of ignoring or neglecting her, and she could not also blame them for maintaining a certain distance from her. Or maybe it was she who drew that circle around her, a circle which she wouldn't allow others to enter.

However strange the situation, they had taken her in when her parents had 'deposited' her into their home when she was barely seven years old. The arrangement was supposed to be temporary, while her dad and mom sorted things out in their lives. It became easier to bond with Ando at that time, who was just her age. There was no awkwardness because both of them were awkward enough alone.

She may not have distinct memories of her room, but Cecilia now has to admit there are still memories about that family that stand out. She remembers how she secretly pined for Mario's attention. He was two years older than her and Ando, and she would have moments of sweetness directed at her as a younger sister. But when she was in high school and he in college, he became aloof. He was always out with his friends. Ando told her at the time that Mario already had a girlfriend, and to punish Ando for this news that had saddened her, she hadn't talked to him for days. She believed then that Ando intentionally wanted her to know and be hurt about the presence of a girlfriend in Mario's life.

The summer before she entered high school and Mario went to college, she convinced herself that Mario somehow felt something for her. The whole family went on vacation in Siquijor Island to celebrate the triple graduations—she and Ando from Grade 7 and Mario from high school. She was not in a celebratory mood because of talk about the beach. The last time she had been on a beach on a summer vacation had been painful for her. Her biological father had taken her to a vacation in his hometown in Quezon province so she could meet his side of the family. She had thought this meant he was taking her back and they would be together again. But after that short trip, he had brought her back to her adoptive family, and she had given up on that hope. It had occurred more than two years after both her parents had first left her with their closest friends. By the time the Siquijor trip was proposed, that summer with her father seemed to her to have been a long, long time before.

On the boat trip to the island she made a mess when she

threw up breakfast and had to lay her head on Ando's shoulder because the slightest movement gave her vertigo. She felt comfortable using Ando's shoulder and it didn't embarrass her that his lap had been the repository of her vomit. But after the rough boat ride, she would turn cruel again and snub Ando when they were touring the island in the afternoon. A tricycle which could take from three to four passengers inside, and another one at the back of the driver, was the only public transportation in the island. The owner of the resort where they stayed had hired two trikes for them to get around. She would have been in the one that her Auntie Ellen and Uncle Lermo rode had it not been for Ando's intervention.

'Us kids should stay together to make this trip more fun,' Ando had said and the remark made sense to Cecilia. She felt happy, yet tried her best not to show her gratitude to Ando. When he sat beside her inside the small vehicle, and Mario had to take the space behind the driver, she didn't feel so friendly towards Ando anymore. Touring the entire island via tricycles would take about four to five hours depending on how long they would want to stay at their stopovers, the drivers had explained. Their first stop was at the centuries-old balete tree, a known tourist site in Siquijor. She could hear Ando's voice right by her ear during the entire trip. When he saw her showing interest in the trees that lined the road, he offered a lecture. He even knew that corn and coconut were staple products of the island. He told her that Siquijor was believed to be enchanted and that they should ask the driver to find them an old woman who could make gayuma, the famous love potion, or a mangkukulam to create a curse on any bullies at school. She almost wanted to slap him. Instead she just gathered all the annoyance she could muster so that Ando could see it writ all over her face. Fortunately for her, Ando finally kept quiet when they stopped at the old churches.

For some reason, Cecilia was glad that her step-parents decided to stop at the San Isidro Labrador Church. They couldn't enter because they were all wearing shorts and slippers, but they could admire the historic structure from outside and take pictures. A girl, probably only a year younger than Cecilia, approached her. Ando kept a distance from her during this time, sulking. He was ignoring her as punishment for her snobbishness.

'Please buy candles from me. You should light candles and say a prayer. I guarantee they will be answered.' The girl pleaded with Cecilia, saying her prayer would be heard, which amused Cecilia. But what the girl had said was more acceptable to her than Sister Adriana's words during their school retreat when she assured her that everything would be fine with her life, her future, if only she kept on praying to God.

'OK, how much?' Cecilia asked the girl.

'One peso for one candle. How many do you want?'

'OK, light five for me.' Cecilia found her coin purse inside her tote bag and handed a five peso coin to the girl, feeling in the mood to be friendly with her.

'What's your name?'

'Mildred!'

'OK, Mildred, light only three candles for me and say a prayer too on my behalf. What do you think I should pray for? And keep the two pesos for yourself, OK?'

'Oh, no, no, I can't do that. That's prohibited.'

'To say a prayer for me?'

'No, to not light all the candles you've paid for and keep the two pesos for myself.'

Mildred then ran towards the side of the church where the candle stand was. Cecilia lost interest in what the girl was doing; let the girl decide what to pray for on her behalf. Just then, Ando approached to tell Cecilia that they would be going.

Their next stop was the famous island's waterfalls. After disembarking from the tricycles, they had to climb down concrete stairs hidden among trees to get to the falls. The folks there said the stairway totaled 200 steps, but after reaching the bottom, Cecilia decided rural folk always exaggerated. The falls and the blue-green river that streamed from it were a sight to behold. Cecilia knew that she couldn't resist going into the water. But she wasn't a good swimmer, and she knew that rivers like this would be deeper and more treacherous, especially directly under the falls. While she was thinking things through, Ando had already plunged into the cold water and waved at her, forgetting how rude she had been to him on the way there. This made Cecilia angrier. She would have preferred for him to continue disliking her. That Ando readily forgot her rudeness to him after he had cared for her during the boat trip was for Cecilia a proof of Ando's childishness. She glanced at Mario who was untying the straps of his sandals after having taken off his shirt. He glanced back at Cecilia and smiled.

'Let's go!' he said.

Surprised by Mario's remark, Cecilia couldn't immediately decide.

'Don't be afraid, I can guide you,' he reassured her.

Cecilia took off her slippers and her white t-shirt, revealing a swimsuit beneath it. She demurred about removing her shorts and immediately climbed down towards a lower rock, right behind Mario. He reached out for her hand upon reaching the water and she landed right beside him. She was aware Ando was watching them.

'Kuya, I'll swim to the falls. There's a nice rock underneath. Come on, let's race. The manong driver said the waters there are the deepest,' Ando called out. He gave Cecilia a mocking look before going under the water, believing that she would be afraid to swim and join them.

'Would you like to go?' Mario asked Cecilia, not minding Ando's challenge. Mario sensed Cecilia's hesitation. 'You know how to swim.'

'I'm not sure. There are rapids here and I am not confident yet.'

'Come on, hold on to my shoulders and swim with me.'

Cecilia looked at Ando who had already reached the huge rock behind the falls and gave him a slight smile, but the scorn in it could not be missed. She felt triumphant upon seeing the expression of defeat on Ando's face. In fact, it seemed to her that he was almost about to cry.

On reaching their destination, Mario wrapped his arms around Cecilia to help her up onto the slippery rock to sit beside Ando. She turned her head slightly towards Mario, so their faces were very close, and smiled at him gratefully. Mario smiled again, while Cecilia felt her heart's hard beating.

She knew that back in the city, Mario would become

aloof again, and then she'd learn again about him getting serious with a girlfriend. But the moment at the falls was enough for Cecilia to think that the prayers given at the church they'd visited had indeed been heard. She couldn't help but be convinced that the island was enchanted after all, and Mildred was her benevolent spirit.

It had been a while now since she had reminisced about Mario and Ando. She had left for the States almost six years ago, agreeing to live with her natural mother and her new family – a husband and his daughter – in New Jersey while finishing college, even though she hated the idea of living with them.

The main reason for going back to the Philippines now is that her father has died. But a dinner with her Auntie Ellen and Uncle Lermo, and Mario's family, is also on her itinerary. Mario is a lawyer and has married. Her adoptive parents still live in the same townhouse. Ando entered the seminary last year and she received the news from Ando himself. She didn't answer his email about his plan to become a priest.

But it had triggered memories of the excursion to Siquijor, of Ando's endless monologues, and finally, of him locking himself in his bedroom when Cecilia was leaving for the airport. He hadn't said goodbye, even when Cecilia had knocked threateningly on his door. She could hear him crying and again she thought he was being immature.

Yet, just last week, after a year of not getting in touch with Ando, it was he she emailed, asking him to tell everyone that she was coming back. She requested that he ask permission from the seminary to take her around, maybe even go to a beach.

After all, he was her first love, even though semi-incestuous relationships are a mortal sin. She jokingly wrote this in her email, adding a smiley icon at the end and addressing him as 'Dear soon-to-be Father Armando'. An independent woman now, she could at last put into sensible perspective the erratic movements of her heart when she'd been such an innocent girl vying for male affection for which she yearned.

THE BARE BONES OF A STORY

David Adès

Abraham slept soundly in his father Yitzhak's cart as their donkey Thuselah walked slowly along the path to a neighbour's farm, the cart laden with vegetables. The neighbour had kindly agreed to help Yitzhak after Abraham was born by taking produce from Yitzhak's farm to the village once a week and selling it for him. All that Yitzhak had to do was get the produce to the neighbour – a walk of half an hour instead of two or more hours. This arrangement, made on a temporary basis after Abraham's birth, had continued for some months.

Abraham slept soundly whilst the cart was unloaded, and slept on whilst Yitzhak and Thuselah walked back to the farm. He slept as Yitzhak unhitched the cart from Thuselah and gave Thuselah a reward for his labour. He slept as Thuselah drank from a trough and was patted down. He slept until the moment Yitzhak took him out of the barn, out of the presence of Thuselah. He woke then with a start and a plaintive cry, a cry that seemed to Yitzhak's ears to be the cry of a great loss, a cry that reverberated in Yitzhak's heart that was itself in the midst of a prolonged and silent keening.

'I hear you little chickchick. You must be hungry. Let me fix some hot milk for you.'

Abraham kept up a weedy whine as Yitzhak busied himself at the grate, getting a fire going, pouring milk into a battered and blackened little pot, stirring it whilst it came to a boil, then skimming the cream off the top and leaving the milk to cool a little.

'Would you like to hear a story, my little one?'

Abraham's whine subsided just a little.

'This is the first story I must tell you, a story that I promised someone I would tell you before any others, and that I promised to tell you over and over, with little variations, so that you would come to know it well.' He stopped for a moment and then, in a low voice that seemed to choke on itself, continued: 'I am a man who keeps his promises.'

'This is a story that is a stream, that becomes many streams. All the streams lead to a river that becomes many rivers. All the rivers in turn lead to the sea. In that sea much is hidden and less is understood. It is here we must all go to learn something of who we are and of the world around us.'

Abraham had fallen silent. Yitzhak stood up and tested the milk. It had cooled enough. He put it in a bottle with a small rubber teat. He bent over and picked up Abraham from his basket and, holding him gently in one arm, put the bottle to his mouth. Abraham looked up at Yitzhak with solemn eyes.

Yitzhak paused a long moment before resuming. 'It is not an easy thing for me to tell you this story. I've left my heart in it somewhere. The story is about a man who was lost. He was so lost that he had not the slightest inkling that he was lost. He did not know that he was lost until he was found. Being found was like being struck by lightning. Having been found, the man found himself. And finding himself, the veils slipped from his eyes and he could see that he had walked the world in blindness. The world was suddenly a brighter place. And then the lost and found man was lost again. Darkness descended. Except that the man was changed. The man knew about the lightning and the blindness, the man knew about the veils. The man was lost again but had the memory of having been found. The man knew that he could not afford to stay lost but did not know the way back to being found.'

Yitzhak stopped for another long moment, lost in his thoughts. Abraham's eyes were fixed upon his father's face. He had nearly finished the bottle, drinking it slowly. Yitzhak was afraid that Abraham would cry again, but Abraham remained silent.

'The man in the story, little one, is your father Yitzhak Yeheskel Zittel. There is a woman in the story and it is to her that I made my promise. Witness now that I begin to keep it, though I didn't know how hard it would be to keep. The woman's name was Zara Zittel, whom I sometimes called Zee Zee and Zittele and many other names beside, for we all have many names, chickele, just as we are all made of many stories. And soon you will recognise from her name, that Zittele was your mother whom I loved and who loved me like no man has been loved. Your mother, whom I have lost (as you too have lost her) and in the losing, lost myself.'

Sometimes a man will speak and a baby will hear the

murmur of its father's voice and it will soothe and lull, and the baby will fall asleep. Abraham's eyes remained wide open, looking up towards the sound of his father's voice, wanting to hear it continue. Yitzhak looked down at his son and felt his joy surge against his sadness. Joy and sadness, what inseparable bedfellows they are. How they tease and play and fight together. How one has the upper hand, and then the other. How they look away from each other, ignore each other, and then fall into each other's arms again.

Yitzhak sighed.

'I know how to tell a story my chickchickee, but I don't know how to tell this one. I have not told it before so forgive me if I pause and shuffle and go tumbling over rocks, so that the story goes where I do not know it will go. It is such a long way to the sea, and there are so many different ways to get there.

'I know that my Zara would tell the story differently, find her own way to the sea in a lovely sing-song voice, that her way would be gentle and direct, and that the story would be both the same story and another story, one that only she could tell.

'What can I say? I was a man who looked at the ground when I walked. I tended my vegetable crops in the ground. I kept my eyes on the ground when I made my trips to the market and back again to make sure that the wheels of the cart didn't get stuck in any of the potholes or ruts. The ground provided me with what I needed to survive. It is not that I was a downcast man, or that I didn't from time to time look up at the sky; it's just that the ground was the natural resting place for my eyes.

'Running the farm by myself, and then with such help as Thuselah was willing to give, took all my attention. I was not a shy man, and I was unafraid, but I was preoccupied with the farm. In a background way, I was aware of the absence of a woman in my life, of the passing of the years and my growing distance from fatherhood, but I did not dwell upon such things and they did not unduly concern me.

'One day I was running late to market. Thuselah was being annoying and, it seemed to me, opportunistically unhurried. Anxious, I tried to push and prod him along, knowing even as I did so that it would only increase his resistance and most probably make my arrival at the market even later. A mistake of impatience from a normally patient man: the type of mistake I endlessly scold myself for (but that is another story). At that exact moment, a wheel of the cart and a rut in the road came into perfect alignment. By the time I arrived at the market it was half over. As I set up my stall and bent down to arrange the boxes of potatoes and sweet potatoes, and other vegetables of the season, I was flustered and dishevelled and hoping very much to salvage something from the day.

'It was at the very moment of maximum distraction and disorganisation that your mother stopped in front of my stall. I looked up to see her standing there, composed, assured. I had never seen her before. She was a stranger to the region who had come to the village in search of work, and she had found a position assisting an elderly couple without children in running their household.

'She was a little woman whom I would later discover was made almost entirely of heart. There was something bird-like about her. Her shoulder blades under her blouse and scarf must be, I thought in that moment when I thought a thousand thoughts, delicate and fragile. When I knew her better, I felt that the lineaments of her bones might almost house wings that could unfurl and lift her into flight. I never knew exactly if she was bird or angel. To me she was both and much else besides.

'Her eyes were the same deep green as yours, and though they were calm and true, there were hints of movement in them, as if all the birds of the forest were gathered there, flittering from tree to tree. It seemed to me as if many things were gathered and concentrated in those eyes. They gathered me in one look and I was lost as I had never been lost and I was found as I had never been found.'

Looking down at last, Yitzhak saw that Abraham had fallen asleep.

In the days that followed, Yitzhak repeated and continued telling the story of his love for Zara to Abraham, noting with interest that Abraham never cried whilst listening to this story, though he often cried when not listening to it. As a result, Yitzhak became an accomplished storyteller and in the years that followed, father and son grew to love both the telling and hearing of stories, whether to one another or to others. What began as the keeping of a promise, became, as Zara had anticipated, a ritual.

The storytelling took place at the end of the day, when both Yitzhak and Abraham were tired – but when Yitzhak had finished all the chores of running the farm, and had spent the day collecting his thoughts, and when Abraham had cried long enough to be ready to stop. In this way, the story told was woven into the stories of the day, the stories of hunger and tears, the stories of the ground, of a recalcitrant donkey and aching muscles, the stories of and from the market, the stories of loss and sadness, the separate and interwoven stories of father and child, the stories of a green forest and a worn track to a village, streams of stories becoming rivers, becoming a sea, becoming a world.

'One day, my little chickska, when you have been made and unmade and made again, I hope you will know for yourself the power of love. I hope you will feel it make you want to become a better man, no matter how good a man you have already become. I hope, of course, what all parents hope for their children: that they will be held in the arms of love, that they will be redeemed, that they will transcend.

'I was not a good salesman that day. There I was, standing at my stall before the woman who would become your mother, with all my vegetables still to sell, open-mouthed and silent with a herd of thoughts galloping around in my head, unable to extend her the least courtesy of a nod or a greeting. A hope I had never acknowledged, a need I hadn't recognised, clamoured for my attention.

'My heart swelled, my ears tingled with anticipation. My body seemed to be in the grip of a strange paralysis, as if it were made of thousands of iron filings desperately resisting the force of a huge magnet. For the first time, I was afraid of a woman. I felt captive. I was afraid that if I moved I would crash into her and be unable to draw back again.

'The angel bird woman spoke: "I don't suppose you have any vegetables here that I might buy," she said, her voice grave and lilting and full of humour all at the same time. I heard an angel speak, and though I knew she was making fun of me, I felt as if I heard a commandment. "Yes, of course," was all I managed to say in reply.

'A long history was contained in your mother's voice, tales of darkness and desperation, tales of theft and redemption, an undeclared love, an unrealised promise, an unknown future. I was unprepared, as men are often unprepared. I hovered on the brink of the abyss, on the brink of the miraculous. And that was how we began our journey to you my chickita, your mother and I, in that first moment of recognition and possibility.

'We were not young when we first met. I was already forty-five years old and Zara was thirty-six. For seven years we made our own history together, our seven years of plenty, our seven years of planting crops, of sowing seeds. We were joyful in our plenitude, the quiet rituals of our days, our nights cupped in each other's arms. We spoke to each other softly, tenderly, the rhythms of the seasons in our voices. We spoke of many things and the world seemed to open more widely, and my sight to attain a new clarity.

'Most of all, we spoke of having a child, perhaps more than one, though time was passing and the prospects diminishing. We held the prospect of a child in our imaginations as we would the reality of a child in our arms. You were wanted, my son, for a long time before you arrived. We shared our doubts but gave each other strength and love and never yielded to despair. At last we were rewarded and my Zittele's body swelled with child. You were coming to us, chickchick, from the faraway place of our dreaming – coming to us like a prophesy fulfilling itself.

'Looking now, I see that there were portents I did not see. For all the newfound clarity of my sight, for all the lifting of veils, for all the sudden brightness of the world, not everything was visible and not everything that was visible was understood.'

Yitzhak stopped speaking. It was late and Abraham had that distant look in his eyes that preceded sleep. Nothing I am saying makes any sense to him yet, thought Yitzhak. I will have to tell him this story again and it won't be any easier.

Yitzhak rocked Abraham gently, and as he did so, rocked himself. He didn't want to tell the story, he didn't want the story to end the way it did, he didn't want to have to repeat it again, and he didn't want to feel all the grief that accompanied the story. The story was a promise, a burden, an obligation, but it was not yet a relief. Perhaps that would come later. In any event, he would not swerve. A promise is a promise, and it must be kept, even in the face of death – especially in the face of death. Abraham was drifting calmly into sleep.

'Perhaps I should tell you the rest of this story, for the first time, whilst you are sleeping, so that you receive it as the murmuring of the sea, so that you receive it as a dream. You can hear it again later, when you are awake. Perhaps I need to tell it to you while you are sleeping, so that when I am overcome with sorrow, when my voice catches and I falter, you will not notice, Abileh of your mother's eyes.'

Yitzhak took one deep breath and then another. He felt the moistness in his eyes, a stab of panic. There was nowhere to be but here, nowhere to go, no place to hide from the keening of his heart. With an effort of will he calmed himself.

'As your mother's body swelled I noticed but didn't understand the marks appearing on her shoulders and back, the appearance of the first white feathers as she became more bird, more angel. Her body was preparing itself for you and preparing itself for something else as well. I asked her about this and her answer was a smile. In the smile I saw a rope with strands of joy and sadness twined together, inseparable. I did not know if the rope was a rope for ascent or descent. I did not know what it meant. But this was the extent of her answer and she did not explain further.

'We prepared for the day of your birth, for your arrival into the world, as parents have prepared for the arrival of children for generations. We readied ourselves, readied the farm, readied our lives, played with our hopes and expectations, and entered into the dream of a family. As we did so, Zara's feathers were becoming wings, translucent, delicate like everything about her, yet strong like everything about her. I looked at her in wonder, and when she met my gaze her eyes reflected my wonder back at me.

'On the day of your birth, Zara drew me close to her. Her voice was soothing, her voice was a lullaby and she was singing to me. Her voice was soothing but her words chilled me. Fear awoke in me again like a chained beast sensing a weakness in the link of a chain and throwing itself forward to break it with power in its hind legs and rage in its mind. "Love of my life," she said, "you have drunk well from the cup of my body that I brought to your lips. My body was a treasure that you treasured as I treasured yours. My body has been the home of your hands and thrilled to their touch. My body has been the hearth of your heart, the palace of your eyes. You have watched as it has grown wings, wings that are for a purpose, wings that must fly. You have had the treasure of my body and you will have my body's greatest treasure. That treasure will sustain you in the days and years to come, my love. But you must make me one promise."

'I was slow to understand, as men are often slow to understand. What was Zara saying? If she could fly from me, why could she not also fly back to me? We had prepared for a future together, not for a future in which she would not be present. She took my hand and pressed it to her heart, to a softness and warmth of breast. "This heart is yours, my love, has always been yours, will always be yours. It asks of you one final promise."

'I nodded slowly, my tongue cleaved to my mouth, my voice lost. "Promise me that you will tell our child our story as soon as you can, and that you will tell it again and again so that the story becomes a part of the child, as the child is a part of the story."

'I made my promise, and now, I have kept the first part of it, though I have told you only the bare bones of it, and I have told it imperfectly, and more as trickle than as stream.'

TAXI DRIVER

Guy Micklethwait

After completing an eight-month round-the-world trip in the early 1990s, I had just arrived back in my adopted home town of Sydney. I was staying with my mate Dave, who lived in a quiet leafy street in Darlinghurst, just off Boundary Street.

'So, now you're back what are you going to do for work?' he asked.

'Get a job as a sales engineer,' I said confidently.

'I thought you tried that before and every company told you to get a year of corporate sales experience before applying again.'

Dave knew that even though I had an engineering degree, they'd said my sales experience working at a timeshare resort wasn't enough.

'So, I get it. That's why you spent the twelve months before this trip selling advertising for a publisher?'

'Yep, and now I am ready to apply again. But those jobs don't grow on trees, so it might take a while to land one, which could be a problem as I've maxed out my credit card.'

'How much do you owe?' he asked.

'Only $8,000.'

'Wow. You put the whole trip on your credit card? Are you mad?'

'Not at all, because I knew when I got back I'd pay it off in no time if I was working as a sales engineer.'

'But you're not, so how are you going to survive in the meantime?'

'I haven't quite worked that out yet,' I said.

'That's so typical of you. Look, it's only a short walk to the Paddington taxi depot from here, so why not visit them and find out how to apply for a cab licence?'

I took Dave's advice, and in no time I was driving a taxi, seven nights a week and was pulling in solid amounts of cash.

Each day I rented a cab for 12 long hours after picking it up soon after 3 pm. On quieter nights, I would be back soon after midnight but on the Friday and Saturday night shifts, I'd keep the cab until 3 am, as those nights were my biggest earners.

The hours worked out perfectly for me, as each day I would sleep in until about 10 am, with any job interviews scheduled for around lunchtime, before I headed off to start my next shift at 3 pm.

I stuck mostly to the Eastern Suburbs, but occasionally was dragged out to Liverpool or the Northern Beaches. It was a great way to discover new parts of Sydney. Although I would receive a large fare for the long trips out, it wasn't good business because more often than not I'd have to drive back into the city empty-handed.

I never waited at taxi ranks but instead spent my evenings cruising around the pubs in Darlinghurst, Paddington and Woollahra because their clientele usually only wanted a short ride to the next pub or back home. Every new customer meant that I got another flag fall, so that's how I maximised my profits.

During the evening part of the shift, I would mostly pick up happy drunks, but late at night I had to deal with heavy drinkers, drug users and all kind of weirdos and trouble-makers.

There was never a dull moment. For example, if a drunk businessman got in the back of my car with a young woman, I could never be sure if they were going to end up shagging or throw up all over my back seat! When the latter occurred, they were never in any state to help me clean it up so the car would stink of vomit for the rest of the shift.

Driving a taxi could also be dangerous. Soon after starting work at the Paddington depot, a couple of the more experienced drivers were chatting with me and gave me a few tips.

'There are certain suburbs where you should never stop at night,' warned one guy.

'And never pick up Maoris,' the other said.

'I'm not a racist,' I replied, 'I'd like to think I'd give everyone a fair go.'

'Looks like you're gonna have to learn the hard way,' they laughed.

I wasn't sure what they meant, but it wasn't long before I found out.

Later that week, I was driving back to the Eastern Suburbs through Redfern which, along with Blacktown, was one of those areas they had warned me about.

The little voice in my head kept saying, 'Whatever you do, don't pick up anyone in the dark,' so I kept going.

On my way out of Redfern, it began to rain. I was driving down a dark road with no houses or streetlights, when up ahead I saw a person on the side of the road next to some dark green bushes waving at me to stop.

Another voice in my head said, 'Look, he's all alone, he could be in trouble.'

'Just keep driving,' came the reply from the other voice.

As I got closer, I could see he was a large man with tattoos.

The first voice piped up again, 'How would you like to be left standing in the rain with every taxi driving past you?'

'Don't be an idiot,' came the harsh reply.

I decided to give the guy a break, so I slowed down and pulled up alongside him. He opened the back door and said, 'Thank you, brother.'

But he didn't get in, he was just standing there holding the door open. I turned around and saw three other Maoris clamber out of the bushes and jump into the back of my cab.

They laughed and joked as they passed around cans of beer and a bottle of whiskey.

Feeling nervous, I asked the guy in the front, 'Where to?'

'The Cross, brother, where else?' he said.

The men were drunk and pushed and shoved each other around, spraying beer all over the place as one of them showed off his latest knife. I could have asked them not to drink in my cab but thought better of it. I didn't say a word until we arrived.

We passed the giant Coca Cola sign and continued along Darlinghurst Road, past a row of strip clubs with a McDonalds wedged in between. We stopped when the driver of the car in front wanted to speak to a hooker on the crowded footpath, so I asked, 'Would you like to get out here?'

'This will do just fine,' one of them said, and they promptly swung open all the doors in unison. They didn't exactly do a runner, they just sauntered off. I leaned out of my open car window and optimistically yelled after them, 'What about the fare?'

One of them looked back. 'Thanks for the ride, brother!' he called out, and they disappeared into the crowd of hookers, pimps and drunken party-goers.

People like this never pay their cab fare and were the type you shouldn't argue with. After that day, I never picked up a fare in Redfern again nor stopped for a Maori at night even though I recognised I was discriminating on racist grounds. I just couldn't afford to take any chances.

Another risk you had driving a taxi was getting robbed, but it didn't always happen at night, and it wasn't always violent.

One Saturday afternoon near Central Station, I picked up a small skinny man with scruffy grey hair. As soon as he climbed into the front seat the strong stench of alcohol hit me, and I couldn't help noticing that the half-open sports bag he had placed between his feet was full of bank notes.

'Taylor Square,' he said as he leant forward to pick up some of the notes that had fallen out.

He saw me glancing down at his bag and said, 'I had a good day at the races, so now I'm off to the pub to celebrate.'

'Looks like you had some major good luck,' I said, trying to calculate in my head how many thousands of dollars were in that bag. He just nodded.

We drove up Oxford Street, and he seemed to be contemplating something. 'I tell you what,' he said, 'I'll share some of my luck with you if you like.'

He dipped his hand into the bag, grabbed a wad of 20-dollar notes and slowly counted them out one by one. It came to exactly $300.

My eyes lit up. 'You're going to pay me $300 for this short trip?'

'No, don't be silly. I'm a gambling man. We have to make it into a bet or it's no fun,' he said.

'What do you mean?' I asked.

'I'll bet my $300 against your change. How much do you have in that coin dispenser?'

'I just started my shift, so only about $40,' I said.

'Okay it's a deal,' he said. 'If I lose I'll pay you a fare of $300, but if I win I get a free ride and you give me your change. Flip of a coin. What d'you say?'

One voice in my head said, 'It's a good deal. You've got a 50/50 chance of winning.'

The other voice interrupted, 'Don't trust him. He's drunk and probably won't pay you even if you win.'

'But if you do win,' came the reply, 'you can take the rest of the day off and have a Saturday night out with the lads.'

I had to make a decision soon, as we were about to arrive.

The temptation proved too much for me.

'Okay, but only if I can toss the coin,' I said.

'Alright,' he replied, 'I get to call then.'

I pulled up outside the pub and grabbed a dollar coin out of my change dispenser.

He checked it to make sure it was legit before passing it back to me.

I tossed the coin upwards, and his eyes lit up as he shouted, 'Heads!' I caught it with my right hand on the back of my left. I lifted my wrist to slowly reveal the coin.

'Damn. It's heads,' I said.

He quickly emptied all my change into his bag before passing me the empty coin dispenser.

'It really is my lucky day,' he said, 'I'll have to play the pokies when I get inside.'

And then he was gone.

Oh well, I thought, I'd better stop at an ATM and get some money out.

It's only $40, I reasoned to myself. It was worth a 50/50 gamble to win $300. You win some, you lose some.

The rest of my shift went smoothly enough, and I arrived back at the depot, returning my car on time. I then walked over to chat with a small group of drivers, who had also just got back. They all fell about laughing when I told them about this weird gambler I had met at the start of my shift.

'He's a con man,' one of them said. 'We've all been caught out by him.'

'You're lucky you only lost $40. I lost a lot more,' said another, as the other drivers poked him in the ribs making fun of him.

'You won't make the same mistake twice,' was their common opinion.

When I got home that evening, my mate Dave was still awake, so I told him about the con artist.

'How do you think he does it?' I asked him.

'Double-sided coin,' he replied. 'He switches it with the original one when he checks it.'

'You're probably right,' I said. 'Well, I won't fall for that trick again.'

Funnily enough, about a month later, I was in Kings Cross, when the same man jumped into my cab with his bag of notes and said, 'Taylor Square please'.

I glared at him. 'You don't remember me, do you?' I asked.

He gave me a strange look.

'You've been in my cab before,' I said. 'You either pay the fare in advance or you take the next cab.'

He opened the door and smiled, 'No worries mate. Plenty more cabs in this city.'

I drove a cab for three months before I finally got that job as a sales engineer. I never ran into that bloke again, but I'd make a bet he's still out there.

A TRAIL OF MARIGOLDS

Geetha Waters

It was October 2017 and I was back in India, staying with a family who ran a school for underprivileged children in the hinterlands of the Deccan Plateau. There were four hundred and sixty children studying at the school, many from the subsistence farms in the local area. These stretched far into the granite hills which lined the horizon. Surrounded by children destined for a hard life with few opportunities open to them due to their caste and financial circumstances, I jostled with ideas of how to improve their education. The question about their future gave rise to the question, 'Are there hidden cultural assets they can draw on?'.

In a country such as India, the transience of life is hard to ignore and I wonder how it affects the human mind. Every few weeks one hears the rhythmic beat of drums heralding a funeral, followed by the sight of pall bearers carrying yet another body covered in white shrouds lying on a make-shift bamboo stretcher. As the latest procession winds its way along narrow lanes, I know it's bound to come past the school where

I'm staying, since the burial grounds are in a thicket of acacias growing in sandy soil just east of the school. From the third storey of my house, I see the procession from far away as the mound of bright orange marigolds piled high over the corpse comes into view. People are walking around the pall bearers, handing the solemn line of mourners orange petals torn from marigolds to throw on their loved one as they take her towards her final resting place.

This time a young woman had died due to the lack of medical care in the area. Perhaps her family had not been able to gather enough funds to take her to hospital in time to save her. In a country with millions of people, such sights are fairly common and few people pause to comment on the causes of life and death. In the past three months, I had witnessed five such occasions. There were many weddings too that I had been invited to. It kept my mind busy with a sense of the relentless onward movement of life. All these people marrying, living and dying, investing so much energy on occasions which were only passages in life. Highlighting a course of priorities that were ritually celebrated by the community seemed to be the only preoccupation which kept people working together.

As the funeral mourners wended their way along the road, I gazed at the young woman's face from my terrace on the third floor, glad that I could maintain a distance from the procession. Her sari shown as pale through the pile of marigold, only her face was revealed to the sky. Her eyes were closed, her face resigned and her lips pressed together in a rigid line of endurance. I wondered if she had had children. Who would look after them? The family walking beside the stretcher were lean, gaunt even. They were all dressed in the customary formal white apparel marking ceremonial occasions in the south of India.

I wondered if her children attended the school where I worked. What did these children make of life and death? The colours of the marigold were many shades of yellow and orange. Their vivid colours spilled over the corpse, falling to the ground as I watched. As they fell on the dusty road on either side of the mourners, they left a trail of petals marking the path in honour of her life. Flowers from the fields which had been picked in the morning by women not unlike the one now lying prone on the stretcher.

I had so many unanswered questions clamouring for attention in my brain, with only humility to contend with as I watched the people with neatly combed black hair walk past under the balcony. Stepping indoors I faced my own mortality. Life is so brief and I did not want to think about people celebrating my funeral one day. It is sad to think about the end of one's life. I wanted to celebrate life with all my heart while I lived. Had this woman felt the significance of her life while being alive? Here she was, absent, when people acknowledged her passing with such pomp and ceremony? Had anyone thanked her for the services she had rendered merely by being part of a community which scrambled to make a meagre living from day to day?

It was obvious that her family had no land to bury her since only those disenfranchised from their lands took their dead to the wasteland at the foot of the eastern hills. It was a good thing that the thorny acacia rambled over the landscape, since they blanketed the graves with their dark green foliage. After the October rains, the whole area was full of sparrows which nested in these bushes, chirping and celebrating their lives during the monsoon when there were plenty of bugs to feed on.

As I shut the door and walked into my flat, I could hear the birds twittering in the bushes below. Chirping mid-flight, they whisked past my windows. The sparrows would swerve and dart in mid-air as they tried to catch the praying mantis that sought shelter in the sprawling green bushes. Just another day and another life which had passed, leaving a family grieving, to get on with their lives as best they could.

I stood by the window a long time, watching the trail of marigolds lining the sides of the road that proceeded towards the burial ground. I watched the granite-capped blue hills that stood stark against the eastern horizon, and thanked my lucky stars that I got to live another day. A feeling of gratitude was the closest thing to the sacred I had encountered. In this land, I needed no ceremony to feel a sense of gratitude. Exposure to the transience of life was sufficient to fill my heart with that feeling.

However, I was glad that our schoolchildren had been spared this occasion. Thankfully it was Sunday, so they did not have to witness yet another funeral going past their school this term.

In the evening the local women would come out into the open from the secluded shelter of their courtyards. They would sweep up the dust along with the withered orange petals in front of their houses, leaving no trace that yet another life had been entrusted to the sacred soil covering the ancient ground of the Deccan Plateau.

Anthology's authors

Stewart Adams

Ever since Stewart read 'Harry Potter' in Year 7, he's wanted to become a writer. In the midst of his work as a firefighter, and being a travel enthusiast and an avid reader, he says he's never short of ideas.

Stewart says he tries to recreate experiences, both real and imagined, 'through the magic of words'.

David Adès

David Adès is an award winning poet and short story writer. He is the author of *Mapping the World* and *Afloat in Light* and the chapbook *Only the Questions Are Eternal*.

David won the Wirra Wirra Vineyards Short Story Prize 2005. *Mapping the World* was commended for the FAW Anne Elder Award 2008. He has also won the University of Canberra Vice-Chancellor's International Poetry Prize, been nominated for a Pushcart Prize and shortlisted for a number of other prizes in Australia and the U.S.

David lives in Sydney with his wife and three children.

Marjorie Banks

Marjorie is a lover of mystery and romance. She combines both these themes in her contribution to the anthology, with a strange tale inspired by visiting an ancient church.

Marjorie is also a keen poet, and as a Sydney-based writer, she is a regular attendee of writing groups at Sydney School of Arts & Humanities.

David Benn

David has a Bachelor of Business from the Queensland University of Technology. Graduating in the midst of a declining economic environment, he moved to Sydney looking for work and briefly followed a career in banking and finance. A redundancy gave him the opportunity to buy a house or travel. David chose to travel.

Now a jeweller in Sydney, David has two sons and is committed to writing in whatever spare time he can find.

Cat Davey

Cat Davey is a former journalist who has previously published two books on finance. She may not have heroically reported on wars or disasters, but she was once bitten by a poodle belonging to Rose Porteous in the course of interviewing her for a magazine article. Cat's interests include both the art and nonsense of fashion, and marsupials, especially the prospect that one day a koala can be a pet.

She also regularly ponders the invention of Google Maps and the usefulness of men from an evolutionary perspective. Her favourite word is stupefaction which she plans to use in her first novel. She lives with her partner, a man with a preference for maps (the expansive folded type), a pair of cats who are sworn enemies and an aged mini foxy called Rex.

Sharon Dean

Sharon is the recipient of a Griffith University Chancellor's Medal for a PhD in Creative Writing. Passionate about working with people whose voices often go unheard, she spent four years running a digital storytelling program that empowered older Australians to share their stories.

A veterinary nurse and animal rights activist, her dream is to create a sanctuary for wildlife and rescued farmed animals on the far north coast of NSW.

Lawrence Goodstone

Lawrence has been writing all his life, albeit for others. With a background in teaching, adult corrections, immigrant services and assisting with the delivery of the 2000 Olympic Games in Australia, he is now writing for himself.

Lawrence has travelled extensively, having worked as a goldminer, a fisherman, a labourer and a factory hand. Now residing with his wife at Bondi Beach, Sydney's iconic beachside suburb, he is in a position to create stories from a life well lived.

Richard Hambleton

Richard has published a number of short stories, and won both first prize and third prize in Victoria's *The Age* Readings Short Story Competition 2013.

He was hired as an advertising writer at the age of 20 and

later built and eventually sold an advertising agency. He now lives with wife Margie in Hepburn Springs, Victoria.

Sam Herzog

Sam is a psychology graduate from the University of Sydney. He had loved reading from a young age and wanted to become a writer, thinking he would need to accrue enough life experience first. On finishing uni, he decided to drop those assumptions and, as he says, 'really commit himself to writing'.

Sam says writing is important to him because it allows him to channel a broad set of disparate interests, and his story in this anthology is one of the first stepping stones on his way to becoming a 'fully-fledged writer'.

Matt Jackson

Growing up in Newcastle, north of Sydney, Matt was described as a boy with an imagination bigger than that allowed by the space in his head. As an adult he splits his time between a professional services career and various creative pursuits.

He writes to explore the raw human experience, and says he seeks to 'challenge the nature of the bond formed between character and reader'.

Grace Lightly

Grace has lived a long and spicy life. Now she secludes herself to write in Rapunzel's tower. Every now and then, she lets her hair down for her youthful muse who climbs up to worship at her temple.

The rest of the time she writes.

Guy Micklethwait

Travel is probably the key to Guy's extensive knowledge and interest in writing. Born and raised in Warwickshire, England, he has travelled to more than sixty countries around the world, including living for a year in Barcelona and another year in Paris.

He completed a PhD in Science Communication at the Australian National University (ANU) before spending a year screenwriting in Hollywood. Moving to China to research an idea for a novel, he found a job teaching Physics in Xi'an.

More recently, Guy has worked in marketing and communications at ANU, CSIRO and as a writer/editor for the NSW Department of Finance, Services and Innovation.

Clarissa Militante

A teacher of literature and creative writing, Clarissa has skills in literary writing in English and Filipino (fiction; creative non-fiction), and editing in English and Filipino. She gained a Master of Fine Arts in Creative Writing from De La Salle University in Manila in 2015 and is currently studying for a PhD.

Clarissa works part-time as a communications officer for 'Focus on the Global South', a non-profit Asian research, advocacy and activist think tank, which has offices in Bangkok and programs in India and the Philippines. It tackles globalisation, investments and trade, climate change and environmental justice, as well as crises in land, water and natural resources.

Jennifer Neil

Jennifer was born in Edinburgh, Scotland, and along with her identical twin sister, was adopted as a baby and taken to South Africa. She became politically active against the apartheid regime there and left in 1960 for England.

She has lived in Australia since 1963 and describes herself as a feminist, lesbian, environmentalist and loving Nana.

Rossco Robertson

Working in IT and graphic design, Rossco dedicates his free time to an eclectic range of passions, from surfing and skateboarding to movies, music, television, pop culture and football. His writing draws on real-life events, chance meetings, and contemporary cultural influences.

He takes as his lode star the adage: 'Write about what you know'.

Rossco has recently had his first sports novel *THE BOOTS* – which is based on elements of Rugby League and the Jedi Knights – published by Sydney School of Arts & Humanities.

Matt Stuart

Ever since he was five when he got up one night to get a drink of water, wandered into the lounge room and unwittingly watched ten minutes of *And Now the Screaming Starts*, Matt has been captivated (and/or irrevocably scarred) by the horror genre.

A many storied collection of careers in education, retail, IT and telecommunications has only strengthened that fascination.

The author of several well-received gaming articles in online publications, this is Matt's first fictional piece to be published.

Carolyn Thrum

Carolyn took up writing following a creative writing course thirty years ago and has been writing ever since. She has edited and published two books of stories written by older Australians and has two of her own stories included in the anthologies.

Carolyn says that for her, the joy is in the writing – getting an idea and building a story around it.

Geetha Waters

Geetha has had two short story collections published by Sydney School of Arts & Humanities, *Road to Rishi Konda* and *Waking the Mind*. Her stories, based on life in India, reflect on the philosopher and radical educator Jiddu Krishnamurti's insight into the mind.

She credits her passion for inquiry as being sparked the first time she heard Krishnamurti speak on education and conditioning to an audience of school students and staff when she was just six years old.